A GARDEN STYLE BOOK

CLIMBING VINES

[SIMPLE SECRETS FOR GLORIOUS GARDENS—INDOORS AND OUT]

MIMI LUEBBERMANN
PHOTOGRAPHY BY FAITH ECHTERMEYER

CHRONICLE BOOKS
SAN FRANCISCO

S

Text copyright © 1995 by Mimi Luebbermann.
Photographs copyright © 1995 by Faith Echtermeyer.
Photographs on pp. 38, 91 copyright
© 1995 by Derek Fell.

Library of Congress Cataloging-in-Publication Data:
Luebbermann, Mimi
Climbing vines: simple secrets for glorious
gardens, indoors and out / by Mimi Luebbermann;
photography by Faith Echtermeyer.
         p.   cm.
"A Garden Style Book."
Includes bibliographical references (p.   ) and index.
ISBN 0-8118-0723-1
1. Ornamental climbing plants. 2. Climbing plants.
I. Title.
SB427.L83 1995
635.9'74–dc20   94-13127
                CIP

Printed in Hong Kong

Cover and interior design by
Aufuldish & Warinner

Distributed in Canada by Raincoast Books,
8680 Cambie Street, Vancouver, B.C. V6P 6M9

10 9 8 7 6 5 4 3 2 1

Chronicle Books
275 Fifth Street
San Francisco, CA 94103

Dedication: To Melinda DeLashmutt
Altshul and Francisco Fuentes-Altshul and
their family, who with such generous
hospitality introduced me to the splendor
of the vines and gardens of El Salvador.

Contents

VINES TO GROW INDOORS 32

VINES TO GROW OUTDOORS IN CONTAINERS 40

VINES WITH AN EDIBLE HARVEST   54

Introduction

Billows of midnight purple clematis floating through an old apple tree, red roses arching over a cottage door, exuberant pink honeysuckle draping a stone wall: These plants adorn our gardens so beautifully because of their special ability to climb and cling. Vines will scale an arbor and soften it with flowers and leaves, unfurl a fragrant ribbon along the top of a wall, or conceal unsightly architectural features quickly and practically. The tracery of vines, the linear look of them, and the luxuriance of their growth add texture and romance to our gardens, walls, and buildings.

¶Vines are simply plants that can grow upward only by attaching themselves to some form of support. The fact that they are so pliable means you can train them into many different shapes. When choosing what vines you want to grow in your garden, consider them as architectural elements. Coax them to grow upward into fans, squares, or triangles, or horizontally to form parallel lines. Select an evergreen vine with dense foliage to surround a pavilion for privacy and a more delicate one to echo the lines of an airy, light-filled porch.

¶Part of the art of gardening with vines is starting out with a vine that suits the space in your garden. Sometimes gardeners have to constantly bully their vines back into shape, for their rampant growth—remember the unruly rose forest guarding the sleeping princess—continually threatens to turn the garden into a jungle. If you've matched the vine to the space available, providing support and gentle trimming is all it will take to enjoy the beauty and bloom of your vine.

¶Vines are wonderfully adaptable. If you have limited garden space or none at all, you can coax vines indoors. A tender vine that could perish in winter's cold will grow in a container; move it inside when night temperatures drop. Out in the garden, vines provide clouds of spring color and fragrance, cooling shade in summer, and fall interest from berries, seedpods, or changing leaf color. Deciduous vines lose their leaves in the winter, but their stems etch otherwise boring expanses of fences and walls in intricate patterns. Vines are practical too, the fast-growing annual varieties will paint over undesirable garden features before midseason.

¶Vining fruits and vegetables are convenient because they save ground space. Pumpkins can be trained to grow up trellises or over walls. Gourds and loofahs will spread along a fence, producing a harvest of old-fashioned birdhouses or bath sponges. Grapes and kiwis smother arbors; beans will race up sunflower stalks to make playhouses for children. Even fruit trees can be grown as vines. Espaliered along south-facing walls in handsome lines, they receive the radiating warmth from the bricks or stone, which encourages fruiting.

¶Local nurseries usually offer a wide range of vines, including hardy deciduous vines from cold regions of the world and tender lush evergreen vines native to the Tropics. Recently, on a visit to El Salvador and Guatemala, I saw many different tropical vines grown together in beautiful walled gardens. The bright blue of the sky, matched by the huge blue butterflies, clashed with the hot pink of the bougainvillea and the canary yellow of the allemanda. The shell pink trumpets of datura peeking over the high stone walls dripped fragrance. The hot colors and rich fragrances made an everyday garden walk an almost hallucinatory experience.

¶*My own garden in Northern California is small and walled, and overlooked on all sides. Although I cannot use the tender tropical vines because we have periods of hard frosts, I try to create the extravagant lushness of tropical gardens. I use rambunctious vines to cover ordinary fences and to create private garden rooms. I have two tall arches that mimic the roof lines, and I am impatiently waiting for them to become clothed with clouds of roses and clematis, which I planted so I'd have bursts of bloom in spring and summer. I let nasturtiums trail like groundcover underneath my fruit trees to cover the fading foliage of the daffodils and provide neon spots of bloom when the trees leaf out and shade the ground. I have shaped a fig tree, as easy to train as any true vine, to be a wall that separates two parts of my garden and provides a honey-sweet harvest. In the street-facing garden, an ugly iron railing is now concealed by the year-round foliage of a trumpet vine. Its summer-long bursts of bloom lure children strolling down the sidewalk, who pluck off the flowers and use them as pretend instruments.*

¶*I cannot imagine my garden with just shrubs and trees. The mystery, romance, and exotic nature of vines have transformed my small square patch of ground into a magical place of color, fragrance, and serenity.*

Characteristics of Vines

Vines are a large and varied family of sprawling annuals and perennials from diverse habitats all over the world. The different environments create very different types of plants. Some are tender to a nip of frost, others hardy enough to withstand Siberian snowstorms. Glossy evergreen varieties form a year-round canopy. Deciduous vines change color and shape through the seasons, their often brilliant fall leaves giving way to a tracery of bare stems in winter.

¶Some dazzle with blankets of spring bloom, and others produce small inconspicuous flowers but prodigious quantities of fruits and berries. Clematis remain as delicate as willowy adolescents, while grapes in their old age grow as mighty as trees with trunks 1 to 2 feet in diameter. Still, among all the differences lies one common characteristic: these plants' inability to support themselves, their need for a structure to climb upon and weave gracefully up into the sky.

¶Vines have developed various means to draw themselves up off the ground toward the light. Darwin, in his *Movements and Habits of Climbing Plants*, examined how a tendril of hop plant twisted 360 degrees around a bit of string in two hours and eight minutes. Twining plants climb either clockwise or counterclockwise, an important distinction. Flanders and Swan, a British song team, composed a popular horticultural parody of Shakespeare's *Romeo and Juliet*, that had the unhappy lovers unable to marry because one family twisted clockwise, the other, alas, counterclockwise. Knowing your plant's twining direction will prevent you from twisting the stem the wrong way and damaging it.

¶Plants like nasturtiums have special leaf petioles called tendrils that encircle anything in sight. Some plants, including climbing hydrangea and ivy, use aerial roots to attach themselves. (Reserve some sympathy for the neighbor who discovers too late that these glue to the sides of houses and can destroy stucco or paint surfaces.) Many of the roses and berries have hooked thorns that grasp or hold.

¶Of course, vines also sprawl over the ground if there's nothing vertical to climb up. For this reason, many vines will do double duty as ground covers, laying a carpet of green with little fuss or muss and, usually, without needing future mowing. Of particular use on steep banks, vines have the merit of looking pretty while preventing erosion.

¶Beware of anyone who airily suggests vines are carefree. Following "just plant them and leave them" advice may result in a cluttered tangle of a garden. However, you can discipline vines, clipping and pruning them to set the shape you desire on a trellis or wall or to create a neat weaving up a tripod of canes.

¶Some vines grow with great vigor. In the late 1800s, kudzu vine, a recent import from Japan, was being extolled as a novelty in gardening books. It was held out as a superior plant for creating shady retreats, combating erosion, and even feeding livestock. Anyone who has been to the southern states in America knows that this demon swallows pastures and clambers over houses and trees, suffocating anything in its path. Look carefully at the growth habit of the vine you wish to settle in your garden, and should you choose one described as "rampant," be prepared to give it room or sharpen your pruning shears.

¶Vines have a curious combination of characteristics: They are both romantic and practical—hardly tendencies that often stroll arm in arm together. Monet created the preeminent romantic garden at his home in France with dreamy clouds of roses on arches and strands of nasturtiums creeping into pathways. The very same plants can paint out an ugly fence or swallow an unsightly shed in soft leafy greens. Perhaps the most special characteristic of vines is that, like a lover's dream, they transform the workaday into the beautiful, which is, is it not, the essence of romance?

About growing vines

What we love about vines is their tractable nature—they will do our bidding, unlike brittle-limbed shrubs and trees. The drawback is that some need guiding, training, and the right type of support. And even the most rampant vines, the ones that twist to the tops of trees in northern hardwood forests or scale light poles in cities without human help, have individual requirements for food, water, and light. Take a little time to understand the growth needs of your vines, so that they'll deliver all the luxuriance and bloom they promise.

¶Most vines grow prodigiously; indeed, the Jack and the Beanstalk fable is worth remembering when planting vines. Generally, vines have very deep roots, which they need both to anchor themselves and to absorb enough nutrients from the soil to keep the foliage and flowers healthy. Dig generous planting holes for your new vines, and mix in plenty of compost so their roots can grow without restraint.

Water

Water carries nutrients from the soil up through the roots and stems to the leaves, flowers, and fruits. As it evaporates through pores in the leaves, the roots draw more water from the soil, like straws sucking up liquid.

¶During periods of high evaporation, such as hot or windy days, the rate of water loss from the leaves increases, so the roots need more water. When the leaves lose more water than the roots can quickly replenish, the plant wilts. A properly watered plant is one that has constant access to readily available water in the soil. During hot and windy days, make sure to increase your watering.

¶Soil composition affects the amount of water available for plants. Very sandy soil drains quickly, so plants have less water available. Clay soils drain less readily. The air in the spaces between the soil particles contains the same gases as our atmosphere; the roots need the oxygen to breathe. When soil is filled with water, oxygen is pushed out and consequently is not available to the roots. Just as plants can die from too little water, they can die from too much. Normally when an area of soil fills with water, gravity pulls the water down through the spaces between the soil particles, allowing oxygen to fill them again. Certain factors, such as heavy clay soils, the lack of a hole in a planting container, or a layer of rocks at the bottom of a planting container, prevent proper drainage and plant roots suffocate. Even though it is traditional to add rocks or crockery to the bottom of containers, they often dam the flow of drainage water, so ignore that century-old instruction and just fill the container with potting soil.

¶Adding plenty of organic matter before you plant is an excellent way to improve soil composition. In sandy soils the organic matter retains moisture; compost absorbs water like a sponge, then holds it available for the plant roots. In clay soils the compost breaks up the clay particles, creating spaces through which water can drain and oxygen can refill. Use your own homemade compost, or purchase aged compost to dig into the soil.

SOILS, POTTING MIXES, AND PREPARED GROUND

Soil is a mixture of the three soil particles—sand, silt, and clay—plus any organic matter. The silt, clay, and organic matter interact with soil water and provide nutrients to the plant roots. Sand, although chemically inert, also plays an important role in plant health. The largest in size of the particles, sand creates correspondingly large spaces between the soil particles, which contributes to fast drainage, high oxygen concentrations, and good vertical water movement.

¶The organic matter in soils is mostly old plant material decomposing under constant attack by bacteria and fungi, which over time liberate mineral elements that are essential to plants for their growth. The bacteria and fungi also benefit plants by fighting off microorganisms that cause plant diseases.

¶You may have seen die-hard gardeners or farmers sniffing the soil; they are checking its quality. Healthy soil crumbles easily in your hand and has a rich earthy smell because of its mix of organic material and soil particles. Your soil should have this good smell, and you should see small bits of decomposed compost among the grains of soil when you look closely. Your spade should slide into the ground easily, and water in a planting hole should drain out slowly but steadily. Good soil produces good plants, so if your plants are not growing well and you do not see signs of disease or insect problems, check with your local nursery about where to have your soil tested.

¶For container plantings, use a good-quality potting mix to ensure it retains moisture, drains well, and does not become concrete hard in late summer. Commercial potting mixes have been sterilized, which makes them cleaner than decomposing materials for growing plants indoors.

¶For outdoor vines, prepare the soil two to three weeks before your seeds or transplants will be ready to set out. If the soil is so wet that it falls off the shovel in clumps, you will have to wait to get started or risk compacting the ground, making it rock hard. First remove existing plant material such as weeds or plants that you no longer want to grow there. Add 4 inches of compost or other amendments, and with a shovel, a spade, or a machine such as a Rototiller, turn the soil over to a depth of 12 to 18 inches. Water the turned soil and allow any undesirable seeds that may be in the ground to sprout. When the ground is damp but not soggy, remove the unwanted plant material once again. Using a hoe or shovel, break up any clods and rake the surface smooth for planting.

FERTILIZERS AND pH BALANCE

The major nutrients needed for plant growth are nitrogen, phosphorus, and potassium. A plant removes these nutrients from the soil and uses them to grow. Adding fertilizer to the soil replaces the missing or used-up nutrients, allowing the plant to continue its growth. Nutrient needs are greatest during periods of rapid growth, typically spring and summer, so these are the best times to fertilize your garden. Commercial fertilizers list their contents as the percentage of each nutrient, in the order nitrogen-phosphorus-potassium. For example, a formula of 10-10-10 has equal amounts of nitrogen, phosphorus, and potassium.

¶Plant growth also depends upon soil chemistry. The pH (potential hydrogen) balance of the soil affects how well a plant absorbs nutrients from the soil. Acid soils have a pH of 6.9 and lower; alkaline soils have a pH of 7.1 and higher. Most vines prefer a neutral to slightly acid soil, but rhododendrons, for example, love acid soils. Purchase an inexpensive kit from a gardening store to test your soil pH, and then learn the pH requirements of your vines. Check with your local nursery for the special products to change the pH of your soil and the fertilizers formulated specifically for acid- or alkaline-loving vines.

¶Plan a regular scheduling of fertilizing. Our garden soil often is no match for a forest floor, where fallen leaves decompose and naturally supply the necessary nutrition to plants. And the many imported exotics we grow may come from soils different than ours and require feeding, somewhat like animals in a zoo, with a supplemented diet.

¶Look for the timed-release low-nitrogen formulas, which provide nutrition for your plants slowly over the growing season. The low-nitrogen fertilizers assist root development and bloom, without excessive foliage growth. Add a small quantity to your planting holes when you set in new plants, and spread a general application over your garden in spring and then again in early summer, following the directions on the package. Stop fertilizing as summer wanes, because you don't want your vines to produce tender growth that will be susceptible to winter's cold.

¶Vines growing in containers need regular fertilizing because there is only a limited volume of soil for their roots and regular watering leaches out the nutrients. Use fertilizers formulated especially for container plants; in addition to nitrogen, phosphorous, and potassium, these also include trace elements and minerals sometimes not added to garden fertilizers.

Starting from Seeds

¶Starting your own vines from seeds is easy, and it offers you the advantage of growing a wide range of varieties that nurseries do not stock. If you live in a cold climate with a short growing season, starting seeds inside produces vigorous plants that are ready for transplanting when the ground warms up. Seeds also can be sown directly into the ground in late spring or summer, after the sun's warmth has brought the ground temperature up to a level that encourages germination. Whether you plan to sow indoors or outdoors, order your seeds in January to make sure you start with fresh, high-quality stock. (Some seed sources are listed on p. 104.)

¶Check at your nursery for the choice of seed starting kits, such as Styrofoam flats, plastic six-packs, or peat pots. Choose pots or containers with individual sections for each seedling so that the transplants will pop out of them easily.

¶Seeds need temperatures of between 65 and 75°F to germinate. Some gardeners place heat mats underneath the germinating trays to keep the soil evenly warm. A sunny south window may provide enough warmth and light. If not, you can hang Gro-lights or full-spectrum lights 4 to 6 inches above the containers. If your plants lean toward the light source and look skinny and weak, they are not getting enough light.

¶Start your seeds six to eight weeks before you want to put plants outside into the ground or into containers. You can buy potting mix or you can make your own formula from equal quantities of vermiculite, perlite, and peat moss. It is important to use a sterilized mix to avoid diseases that infect seedlings. To make sure the plants get off to a good start, add an all-purpose fertilizer to the mix according to the directions on the fertilizer container, or once the seedlings are 1 inch high, water them once a week with a low-nitrogen fertilizer diluted to half-strength.

¶Most vine seeds are fairly large. Soak the seeds from one to three hours before planting or for the amount of time suggested on the seed packet. This short presoaking helps the seeds to germinate, but they will die from lack of oxygen if you soak them too long. Thoroughly moisten the mix with water, then fill the seed container with the mix to within 1 inch of the rim. Check the directions on the seed packet to sow the seeds at the correct depth and spacing. After you have sown the seeds, pat down the mix firmly and water carefully so you don't dislodge the seeds. Keep the mix moist but not soggy to avoid encouraging fungal infections.

TRANSPLANTING YOUNG PLANTS

Because young vines raised indoors or in a greenhouse are very tender, you need to accustom them to the more variable temperatures outdoors before you plant them. For one week before planting, place the young plants outdoors during the day only. Keep them in the shade at first and then gradually move them into the sun. When you plant them, do it in the late afternoon, to lessen the stress caused by the heat of the day.

PLANTING BARE-ROOT PLANTS

Deciduous vines, trees, and shrubs lose their leaves in fall and go dormant over winter. In the very early spring they are sold "bare root," their stems still leafless and their roots loosely wrapped in sawdust and damp newspaper and then encased in plastic. To set bare-root vines in the ground, dig a large planting hole. Add a timed-release, low-nitrogen pelleted fertilizer to the bottom of the hole. Make a pyramid of soil in the bottom of the hole. Unwrap the plant and gently spread the roots over the top of the pyramid, keeping the crown of the plant at soil level. Return the soil to the hole, adding some compost at the same time and making sure that the soil covers all the roots. Tamp down the soil and water thoroughly to prevent air pockets. Add more soil if necessary to cover the roots and keep the crown at soil level.

PLANTING CONTAINER PLANTS

In prepared garden soil that is thoroughly moist, dig a hole for each plant that is at least twice as wide and twice as deep as the container. Add some timed-release low-nitrogen fertilizer to the bottom of the hole. Tip the container over on its side and gently tap out the plant. If the roots encircle the root ball, straighten them out, disturbing the root ball no more than you have to. Set the plant into the hole. Return the soil to the hole, adding some compost at the same time and making sure that the soil covers all the roots and that the stem sits at the same level as it was in the container, at the soil level or slightly higher. Tamp down the soil and water thoroughly to prevent air pockets. Add more soil if necessary to cover the roots and keep the crown at soil level.

HOW VINES CLIMB

Vines have a clever bag of tricks designed to get their soft young stems climbing upward off the ground toward the light. Some twine; they grow around and around whatever support is available. Notice which way they twine, because some turn

clockwise, some counterclockwise, and if you try to turn the vine the wrong way, you may break the growing stem.

¶Other vines put out tendrils, and it is these extra arms of the plant, not the growing stem, that entwine a pole or fence and anchor the plant. Still another group of vines, including ivies, have roots that grow along the stem and glue the plant to a vertical surface. The last group of true vines have no climbing tricks; they'll stay grounded unless you assist them.

CHOOSING A VINE

There are hundreds of vines available in nurseries and mail-order catalogues, but the process of choosing a vine can be quickly pared down by focusing on the best vines for your site and purpose. Check first the amount of space you have available, for if you have only a small area, you can cross off the list all the rambunctious varieties. Wisteria grows huge, heavy limbs that will bring down a small trellis in a couple of seasons. Bougainvillea has been known to swallow charming courtyards, forcing the owners to spend their weekends whacking it back to create enough space to walk from the street to the front door. Choosing a vine that matches the location will save you from adding a gardener to your staff, because in the right location a plant has plenty of room to grow and doesn't need constant attention.

¶If you have a particular function in mind for the vine, you can limit the choice further. For example, if the vine needs to cover up an unsightly building or enclose an area for privacy, you will probably want an evergreen vine, and therefore you can cross deciduous varieties off your list.

because insufficient light will reach the interior. Thin out vigorous growth so that all the remaining stems are exposed to light and will leaf out thickly.

¶Shape your vines to the form you prefer. Cut out stems that cross from one side of the plant to the other; also prune out any deadwood, because it encourages insect damage or infection. Pinching off the very tips of the stems will, for the moment, stop the plant at that height and force out stems lower down, giving you a bushier, fuller-looking plant.

¶Know when it is appropriate to prune your vine. Pruning flowering vines in the spring before they bloom will deprive you of all the blossoms you were expectantly awaiting. After blooming, many vines produce delightful seedpods, which you wouldn't want to miss either. For example, pruning a rugosa rose after flowering automatically ends your chance of a harvest of rose hips in the fall.

FROST PROTECTION

Tender and hardy are the two main words tossed around by gardeners in discussions about how well a plant withstands frost. Tender plants do not like cold temperatures, and a freeze will kill them. Pumpkins are tender; a frost will cause them to shrivel up and die. Hardy plants stand up to the cold, and are often described as hardy to a certain temperature, such as "hardy to 32°F." Half-hardy plants usually survive a short cold spell, but not extended cold spells.

¶Gardeners in cold-winter climates often long to grow tender beauties from the Tropics. This yearning is not new. In European castle gardens there are fireplaces set in hollow garden walls to warm tender plants grown against the outside. Fortunately, there are some simpler ways to protect tender vines in all but the coldest winter gardens.

¶Plant your less hardy vines in the most protected spots in your garden. South-facing freestanding walls stay relatively warm because they absorb the winter sun. South-facing walls under the roof line of a building are usually even warmer and often the most protected spot in the garden. Mulch your vines heavily just before the frost season begins, spreading as much as 2 feet of straw or compost over the base of the plants.

¶You also have the option of growing vines in containers and in fall moving the containers inside to a sunny porch or west-facing window until the temperature comes back up in the spring.

Repotting Vines in Containers

Every two or three years, repot your vine. Withhold water for a week to let the root ball dry out slightly. Trim back the plant to make it manageable, then carefully tip the plant out of the container onto a piece of canvas or plastic. With a sharp knife, cut 1 to 2 inches from the sides and base of the root ball, less if the container is smaller than 5 gallons. Add fresh potting mix to the bottom of the container, slip the root ball back so that it sits 2 inches below the rim of the container, and add more fresh mix around the sides so the plant is centered in the container. Tamp down the sides firmly and water the container thoroughly. Add more planting mix until the mix is level with the top of the root ball. Once a month, fertilize with a low-nitrogen fertilizer formulated especially for container plants.

V I N E S

T O G R O W

I N D O O R S

The Victorians loved their indoor gardens, turning their best parlors into junglelike accumulations of treasured plants. The housekeeping books written at that time contain illustrations  of window gardens with a rustic string of hanging baskets and a thicket of container plants on platforms and shelves. The Victorians cluttered their mantelpieces with bric-a-brac, and even dining-room mirrors were fitted with a soil box in the back so that ivy vines fringed the mirror. ❧ You may eschew quite such excesses, but growing vines indoors does add a ruffle of "verdure," as the Victorians would say. Besides greening your home, indoor gardens provide a winter resort for tropical vines that need protection from the cold weather and a place to putter for gardeners without outdoor gardening ground. There are challenges to fitting a vine into the sheltered environment of the home, not the least being watering it sufficiently without tracing water rings on a rug or wooden floor. For successful indoor gardens, you need to consider light, humidity, and temperature. ❧ Make sure that the light level is appropriate to the needs of your vine. Your windows may be ultraviolet impervious, in which case it will not be receiving the light it needs. Check that you fulfill its humidity and temperature needs. Begin a program of regular watering and fertilizing, using a low-nitrogen fertilizer specially formulated for container plants. ❧ Move your vine around to different light environments if it seems unhealthy. Once a plant flourishes, watch it carefully as the seasons change, because as the sun sets a different course in the sky, the light may diminish in that spot or become too bright and hot. ❧ You may be discouraged if you bring a new plant home and within a few weeks it seems to falter, even with flawless nurturing. Your plant may have just arrived at the nursery from a greenhouse or specialized environment, and it may need to adjust. If worst comes to worst and the plant dies, take the plant back to the nursery and ask them to diagnose the problem.

IVY TOPIARY

There are gardeners who grow flowing borders filled with blooms of rainbow colors, who prune hedges into intricate, stately shapes, who espalier everything from rhododendrons to pears. These selfsame gardeners shamefacedly confess they cannot grow a twig indoors. They shouldn't be so dismayed, for growing plants inside can require fiercer concentration than any type of outdoor gardening, unless, that is, you choose ivy. ¶ Ivy is easy. Even in doctors' offices and the corporate corridors, ivy grows with steady fortitude. It is a hard-working plant, yet has an interesting diversity of leaf size, shape, and color. The small-leafed types are delicate. The variegated dark-green-and-white ivies contrast with those that sport forest green leaves mottled with chartreuse. Try growing combinations of colors and leaf shapes.¶ You can hack away at ivy with no terrible consequences. Try training it as a bonsai, growing several up a wire pyramid as an everlasting Christmas tree, or simply letting it drape gracefully from a hanging basket. You can purchase topiary frames from florist supply shops or florists. ¶ A message to gardeners who would plant ivy outside: To call ivy purposefully malicious would be to ascribe human characteristics to a plant, but be advised that the little furry roots on ivy stems can be destructive. They have a way of squeezing into cracks, which as the stem thickens creates havoc on shingle and wooden buildings. ¶ **HOW TO DO IT** ¶ Choose a topiary frame and three ivy plants. Before planting, submerge the containers in a sink or bucket of water until air bubbles cease to appear. Fill a 20-inch-wide container with thoroughly moist potting mix to within 2 inches of the rim. Remove enough of the mix to make a hole large enough for each plant. ¶ Gently remove a plant and its potting mix from the container and set it in the hole so that the top of the root ball is just at soil level. Fill the hole with potting ✒

Ivy
Hedera helix
❧

What You Need
3 ivy plants
20-inch-wide container
Potting mix
Topiary frame
Plant ties
Low-nitrogen liquid fertilizer
formulated for container plants
❧

Hardiness
Hardy
❧

Growing Conditions
Bright light, no direct sun
❧

Climbing Method
Clinging roots on stems
❧

When to Plant
Anytime
❧

When to Prune
As necessary to control growth
❧

When Blooms Appear
No blooms
❧

mix, packing it gently around the roots. Pat down the surface and water to fill in any air pockets. ¶ Sink the topiary frame carefully into the container. Guide the ivy stems to the frame with ties until they fasten on. Keep the mix moist but not soggy, and fertilize every month with a low-nitrogen liquid fertilizer formulated for container plants. ¶ Pinch back the tips of the plants to encourage branching. As your ivies grow, trim them to a tidy shape. Place the pot in a brightly lit room but out of direct sun.

POTATO VINE

The flower clusters reveal the ancestry of this lacy vine. Like many other members of the Solanaceae family, including potatoes and eggplant, it has five-petalled, star-shaped flowers with bright yellow centers. Its old-fashioned name is Flore de San Diego, which better suggests its delicate and romantic nature. In mild-winter areas, you see this vine outdoors draped over fences and pergolas, and anywhere the gardener wanted a quick easy-care vine with a long season of bloom. ¶ As a container plant, the potato vine lives contentedly indoors in a bright, sunny space. Find a setting where it receives morning sun and you will be rewarded with blooms throughout the spring and summer. Don't be afraid to do year-round pruning. This vine will present a tangle if you neglect it. Guide the new stems where you want them, and don't worry about trimming the plant back to fit your space, because pruning encourages new growth and continued bloom. ¶ **HOW TO DO IT** ¶ Before planting, submerge the container in a sink or bucket of water until air bubbles cease to appear. Fill a 24-inch-wide container with thoroughly moist potting mix to within 2 inches of the rim. Remove enough of the mix to make a hole large enough for the plant. ¶ Gently remove the plant and its potting mix from the container and set it in the hole so that the top of the root ball is just at soil level. Fill the hole with potting mix, packing it gently around the roots. Pat down the surface and water to fill in any air pockets. ¶ Insert two 6-foot stakes or a wire cylinder. Weave the stems up the climbing support. Keep the mix moist but not soggy, and fertilize once a month with a low-nitrogen liquid fertilizer formulated for container plants. To make the container more attractive, cover the soil surface with sphagnum moss. ¶ As the vine grows, pinch back some growth to keep the plant looking tidy. Prune out older stems to allow new ones to grow. Cut off spent blooms unless you like the look of the berries that follow.

Potato Vine
Solanum jasminoides 'Album'

What You Need
Container plant
24-inch-wide container
Potting mix
Two 6-foot stakes or a wire cylinder
Plant ties
Low-nitrogen liquid fertilizer
formulated for container plants
Sphagnum moss, optional

Hardiness
Indoor hardy

Growing Conditions
1/2 day of direct sun

Climbing Method
Twining stems

When to Plant
Anytime for indoor growing

When to Prune
As necessary to control growth

When Blooms Appear
Spring to fall

Carolina Jessamine

The name of this evergreen vine brings to mind southern summer evenings fragrant with the perfume of flowers. In truth this is a little less than accurate, for Carolina jessamine blooms late winter and early spring. By summer its fragrant yellow trumpets have faded, but its bright shiny green leaves are so handsome that the vine will dress up a light hallway or inside porch whether it is in bloom or not. ¶ Carolina jessamine is a good plant for indoors because of its easy-growing nature. Water it regularly. Though it will go some time without, the leaves look crisper with water. Make sure to prune it after the flowers are finished, cutting out older stems and keeping it to the height you wish. ¶ Just a word of caution: Like many other garden plants, Carolina jessamine has leaves and flowers that are poisonous if eaten.

¶ **HOW TO DO IT** ¶ Before planting, submerge the container in a sink or bucket of water until air bubbles cease to appear. Fill a 24-inch-wide container with thoroughly moist potting mix to within 2 inches of the rim. Remove enough of the mix to make a hole large enough for the plant. ¶ Gently remove the plant and its potting mix from the container and set it in the hole so that the top of the root ball is just at soil level. Fill the hole with potting mix, packing it gently around the roots. Pat down the surface and water to fill in any air pockets. ¶ Insert two 6-foot stakes or a wire cylinder. Weave the stems up the climbing support. Keep the mix moist but not soggy, and fertilize once a month with a low-nitrogen liquid fertilizer formulated for container plants. To make the container more attractive, cover the soil surface with sphagnum moss. ¶ As the vine grows, pinch back some growth to keep the plant looking tidy. Prune out older stems to allow new ones to grow. Cut off spent blooms.

Carolina Jessamine
Gelsemium sempervirens

What You Need
Container plant
24-inch-wide container
Potting mix
Two 6-foot stakes or a wire cylinder
Plant ties
Low-nitrogen liquid fertilizer
formulated for container plants
Sphagnum moss, optional

Hardiness
Indoor hardy

Growing Conditions
½ day of direct sun

Climbing Method
Twining stems

When to Plant
Anytime for indoor growing

When to Prune
As necessary to control growth

When Blooms Appear
Late winter to early spring

VINES TO
GROW OUT-
DOORS IN
CONTAINERS

Vines left in the ground to grow at will can swallow trees and overrun tiny gardens, but many grow sedately once ensconced in containers. With its limited root space, a container restricts vine size. ❧ For those in cold-winter areas, growing vines in containers means you can experience the beauty of frost-tender tropical varieties, moving the containers inside or to a sheltered outside area to overwinter. ❧ The right size of container is essential, the general rule of thumb being that the larger the container, the larger the vine will grow. Remember that plants like to be moved into larger containers gradually; as your vine outgrows its 1-gallon container, move it into a 5-gallon one, not a 10-gallon one. ❧ Plan and prepare a climbing structure before your vine starts to grow. Try the commercially available 4-foot wire cylinders, make your own wire cage, or position the container near a wall trellis. If the vine needs tying, make sure to loop the ties loosely around the stems so that as they grow and thicken the ties will not cut into them. ❧ Keeping the containers correctly watered is the most difficult aspect of growing vines this way, because the plant's roots have less soil volume to draw upon for water. Water on a consistent schedule. Before watering, check with your fingertip that the potting mix is only damp, not still soggy. Water more often when temperatures exceed 80°F. Fill the watering saucer with gravel or marbles so that the bottom of the container never sits in water, which encourages root rot. ❧ The better-formulated potting mixes have a texture and composition that help water soak in and drain thoroughly. These mixes usually have a low concentration of soluble salts, which in high doses injure plants. Choose a specially formulated acidic potting mix for vines preferring that formula. Mulch the top 2 inches of the container with sphagnum moss or straw as an additional means of retaining moisture. ❧ Regularly add a low-nitrogen liquid fertilizer specially formulated for container plants to keep your vine growing well. A healthy plant is more resistant to insects and disease.

A HANGING BASKET OF NASTURTIUMS

Nasturtiums are a handy tool for the gardener who has a partly shady spot in the garden or on a deck and wants a fanciful hanging container. The flowers come in deep burgundy, flashing red, yellow, cream, and orange—"peach-melba colors" one company calls them. Some of the new varieties flaunt white-speckled leaves. Grow a mix of colors for a lush trailing bouquet among the cheerful, saucer-sized leaves. ¶ Besides looking fanciful in your garden, nasturtiums can be put to good use. Both the flowers and leaves of nasturtiums are edible. If you run short of salad ingredients, you can pick and munch the blossoms and the youngest leaves for a peppery green. Some gardeners even collect the small seeds and pickle them for a caperlike accent. Kids love to pretend the blossoms are fairy hats, or to set a doll's table with the little round leaves. You can entertain them by stringing the blossoms into necklaces and crowns. Picking the flowers encourages the plant to keep blooming; if you have no other use for them, gather them for charming cut flowers. ¶ You can tell from their crunchy stems that nasturtiums appreciate water, so water frequently. If aphids attack the plants, simply spray them off with a jet of water and respray as necessary. Do not use an insecticide because you never can tell when children will eat up a blossom before you have a chance to stop them! ¶ Your hanging basket of nasturtiums will bloom until fall. If you wish, you can then remove the plants, sow new seeds and continue to water and fertilize. In mild-winter climates, nasturtiums bloom outside all year long. In frosty areas, bring your hanging basket inside and with enough sunlight and warmth, the plants will continue to provide cheerful blooms and foliage throughout the winter. ¶ **HOW TO DO IT** ¶ In the spring, after the last chance of frost, you can sow your seeds directly in the basket outdoors. Prepare a 14-inch wire hanging basket for planting: Line the basket with a layer of sphagnum moss at least 2 inches thick over the bottom and up the sides. Then fill the basket with thoroughly moist-

Nasturtium
Tropaeolum majus
❧

What You Need
Seeds
14-inch wire hanging basket
Sphagnum moss
Potting mix
Low-nitrogen liquid fertilizer
formulated for container plants
❧

Hardiness
Tender
❧

Growing Conditions
1/2 day of direct sun
❧

Climbing Method
Tendrils
❧

When to Sow
After the last chance of frost
❧

When to Prune
As necessary to control growth
❧

When Blooms Appear
Summer to fall
❧

ened potting mix, packing the mix gently until it is even with the top of the basket. Water the basket thoroughly. ¶ Soak ten seeds for one to three hours before you plant them. Bury the pre-soaked seeds 1 inch deep in the potting mix, spacing them around the perimeter of the basket. Gently pat down the mix over the seed and water to fill in any air pockets. Seedlings emerge in six to eight days. ¶ Hang the basket where it will receive bright morning and midday sun. Keep the mix moist but not soggy, and fertilize once a month with a low-nitrogen liquid fertilizer formulated for container plants.

Jasmine

Jasmines are famous for their fragrance, and deservedly so. Memories of long-gone warm evenings heavy with jasmine scent last forever, returning with just a whiff from a florist's bouquet. Place one container of jasmine on a deck or small terrace and drifts of its rich, sweet perfume will float over the air for several months. Having your plant in a container allows you to move its fragrance to just where you want it. The luxuriant scent escapes from the pretty two-tone tubular flowers, white inside and burgundy-pink outside. ¶ Jasmines tend to be on the wild, vigorously growing side, and to keep your plant looking graceful, you need to prune out the heavy entangling growth after it has bloomed and then again at the end of the summer. Jasmine looks lovely with small annuals hanging over the edge of the container. Team it with the pink or white alyssum that blooms at about the same time. ¶ **HOW TO DO IT** ¶ In the spring after the last chance of frost, you can safely plant your new vine. Before planting, submerge the container in a sink or bucket of water until air bubbles cease to appear. ¶ Fill a 24-inch-wide container with thoroughly moist potting mix to within 2 inches of the rim. Remove enough of the mix to make a hole large enough for the plant. To the bottom of the hole, add a small amount of a good-quality timed-release low-nitrogen pelleted plant food, following the directions on the package. ¶ Gently remove the plant and its potting mix from the container and set it in the hole so that the top of the root ball is just at soil level. Fill the hole with mix, packing it gently around the roots. Pat down the soil surface and water to fill in any air pockets. ¶ Use a 4-foot wire cylinder for the climbing structure. Carefully sink it into the container, spreading out the legs evenly. If the cylinder seems like it may topple, weave three evenly spaced garden stakes through the wire cylinder down into the soil. ✐

Jasmine
Jasminum polyanthum
❧

What You Need
Container plant
24-inch-wide container
Potting mix
Timed-release low-nitrogen
pelleted plant food
4-foot-tall wire cylinder or
5-foot-tall wire cage
3 stakes, if necessary
Low-nitrogen liquid fertilizer
formulated for container plants
❧

Hardiness
Tender
❧

Growing Conditions
1/2 day of direct sun
❧

Climbing Method
Twining stems
❧

When to Plant
Spring to late summer
❧

When to Prune
After summer bloom and again in fall
❧

When Blooms Appear
Spring to summer
❧

Alternatively, erect a 5-foot-high wire cage that sits on the ground and encircles the container. Measure how much wire you need to completely encompass the container. Cut a piece that size and with wire or string tie the ends together to form a circle. ¶ Keep the mix moist but not soggy, and fertilize once a month with a low-nitrogen liquid fertilizer formulated for container plants. ¶ In the fall, place the vine in a protected porch or indoor where it will not be damaged by frosts. Continue to water the vine during the winter. In the spring, when the weather has warmed, you can move it outside again.

Black-eyed susans

This old-fashioned country casual flower is usually seen rambling over fences, covering the dullest structures with black-eyed, shiny-bright flowers that are sometimes orange, sometimes white, and sometimes a creamy color. It is very well mannered, easy to control, and adapts to container culture with a minimum of fuss. Gardeners growing this vine swear it takes on a perky personality, and they find themselves almost saying good morning to it. ¶ City dwellers with small gardens or rooftops can use the backdrop of a fire escape or banister for a climbing support, tying the stems upward. Though black-eyed Susan will climb up if tied, it really likes to trail downward. For a cheery window box, mix a tumbling black-eyed Susan with other annuals. Even alone, it presents a very pleasing portrait. ¶ Make sure to find a sunny spot for this vine and keep up a regular watering schedule. There is a perennial species, but it lacks the appealing black centers that give the little flowers of black-eyed Susan so much homely personality. ¶ **HOW TO DO IT** ¶ In the spring after the last chance of frost, you can safely sow seeds directly in a container outdoors. Soak the seeds for one to three hours before you plant them. ¶ Fill a container that is at least 14 inches wide with thoroughly moist potting mix to within 2 inches of the rim. Bury about eight presoaked seeds 1/2 inch deep in the potting mix, spacing them around the perimeter of the container. Gently pat down the mix over the seeds, and water to fill in any air pockets. Seedlings emerge in seven to ten days. ¶ Place the container in a sunny location. Keep the mix moist but not soggy, and fertilize once a month with a low-nitrogen liquid fertilizer formulated for container plants. ¶ If you are training plants up, insert a 4-foot wire cylinder and weave the stems through the structure to get them started. The vines will hang over the sides of a window box or planter without any assistance.

Black-Eyed Susan
Thunbergia alata

❧

What You Need
Seeds
14-inch-wide container
Potting mix
4-foot wire cylinder, optional
Low-nitrogen liquid fertilizer
formulated for container plants

❧

Hardiness
Tender

❧

Growing Conditions
1/2 day of direct sun

❧

Climbing Method
Twining stems

❧

When to Sow
After the last chance of frost

❧

When to Prune
As necessary to control growth

❧

When Blooms Appear
Summer to early fall

❧

Hyacinth beans

Garden plants face as much competition as do cars or corporate presidents. Styles change and gardeners discover plants that are new and fashionable. Although collectors work hard to keep heritage varieties going by saving seeds and plants, old garden books extol the virtues of many plants no longer available. Hyacinth beans might have been one of these has-beens if plant lovers hadn't rescued them from obscurity after their peak of popularity in turn-of-the-century gardens. ¶ Hyacinth describes a color, a deep blue-red, but words do not do justice to the intensely bright burgundy, almost horn-shaped beans that follow the clusters of richly fragrant purple flowers. ¶ Although they will grow well in the ground, do not relegate hyacinth beans to the vegetable garden. Grow them in a large container right out the back door so you can see them burst into purply bloom and then form clusters of baby beans. Besides, when the beans are ready to harvest, you won't have far to go to pluck them and pop them into the pot. Sadly, on cooking the purple fades, but the little beans are tender and fresh tasting. ¶ In the fall when the vine dies down, it leaves tuberous roots that will overwinter if you protect them from frost. ¶ **HOW TO DO IT** ¶ In the spring after the last chance of frost, you can safely sow seeds directly in a container outdoors. Soak the seeds for two days before you plant them. ¶ Fill a container that is at least 24 inches wide with thoroughly moist potting mix to within 2 inches of the rim. Bury the presoaked seeds 1 inch deep in the potting mix, spacing them 4 inches apart around the perimeter of the container. Gently pat down the mix over the seeds, and water to fill in any air pockets. Seedlings emerge in ten to fourteen days. ¶ Use a 4-foot wire cylinder for the climbing structure. Carefully sink it into the container, spreading out the legs evenly. If the cylinder seems like it may topple, weave three evenly spaced garden stakes through the wire cylinder down into the mix. ✒

Hyacinth Bean
Dolichos lablab
❧

What You Need
Seeds
24-inch-wide container
Potting mix
4-foot-tall wire cylinder or
5-foot-tall wire cage
3 stakes, if necessary
Low-nitrogen liquid fertilizer
formulated for container plants
❧

Hardiness
Tender
❧

Growing Conditions
1/2 day of direct sun
❧

Climbing Method
Twining stems
❧

When to Sow
After the last chance of frost
❧

When to Prune
As necessary to control growth
❧

When Blooms Appear
6 to 8 weeks after planting
❧

Alternatively, erect a 5-foot-high wire cage that sits on the ground and encircles the container. Measure how much wire you need to completely encompass the container. Cut a piece that size and with wire or string tie the ends together to form a circle. ¶ Guide the young beans up the climbing structure. Keep the mix moist but not soggy, and fertilize every two weeks with a low-nitrogen liquid fertilizer formulated for container plants. ¶ If you wish to save the roots for growing next year, in the fall place the container in a protected porch or somewhere where the roots will not be damaged by frosts. Continue to water the container during the winter. In the spring, when the weather has warmed, new stems will emerge.

Morning glories

Morning glories make one think of cheerful cottage gardens with spears of delphiniums, bright spots of iris, and, of course, a bower planted with blue, pink, and deep magenta morning glories. The problem for many urban gardeners is that cottage gardens need to be squeezed onto balconies and fire escapes, little back decks, or roof gardens. ¶ Morning glories will bloom prolifically in a largish container fitted with a wire cage if as the vines reach the top of the cage you remove the ends of the stems. Either pinch off the very ends with your fingers or use scissors to cut nice lengths of stems for cut flowers. Morning glories love the sun so grow them in the warmest place you have. ¶ **HOW TO DO IT** ¶ In the spring after the last chance of frost, you can safely sow seeds directly in a container outdoors. Soak the seeds for twenty-four hours before you plant them. ¶ Fill a container that is at least 24 inches wide with thoroughly moist potting mix to within 2 inches of the rim. Bury the presoaked seeds ½ inch deep in the potting mix, spacing them 4 inches apart around the perimeter of the container. Gently pat down the mix over the seeds, and water to fill in any air pockets. Continue to water as needed to keep the mix moist but not soggy. Seedlings emerge in seven to ten days. ¶ Use a 4-foot-tall wire cylinder for the climbing structure. Carefully sink it into the container, spreading out the legs evenly. If the cylinder seems like it may topple, weave three evenly spaced garden stakes through the wire cylinder down into the mix. Alternatively, erect a 5-foot-high wire cage that sits on the ground and encircles the container. Measure how much wire you need to completely encompass the container. Cut a piece that size and with wire or string tie the ends together to form a circle. ¶ Guide the young vines up the climbing structure. Keep the mix moist but not soggy, and fertilize once a month with a low-nitrogen liquid fertilizer formulated for container plants.

Morning Glory
Ipomoea tricolor
❧

What You Need
Seeds
24-inch-wide container
Potting mix
4-foot-tall wire cylinder or
5-foot-tall wire cage
3 stakes, if necessary
Low-nitrogen liquid fertilizer
formulated for container plants
❧

Hardiness
Tender
❧

Growing Conditions
A full day of direct sun
❧

Climbing Method
Twining stems
❧

When to Sow
After the last chance of frost
❧

When to Prune
Only as necessary to control growth
❧

When Blooms Appear
Summer to fall
❧

CLIMBING LILIES

The climbing lily is quite unlike the aristocratic lilies that hold sway over garden beds. Easily grown in a container, this snazzy and sassy species climbs up 6 feet, then bursts out in flower. The splashy blooms have stripes of sizzling red and yellow. ¶ Sometimes climbing lily bulbs are hard to find. Check in late winter or early spring with your favorite nursery so they will order them and save some bulbs for you when they arrive. The bulbs are listed in mail-order catalogues, but order them before they sell out. ¶ Climbing lily bulbs are frost tender, so treat them much like dahlias, protecting them from cold by moving the container to a protected spot for the winter. Just a word of caution: Like many garden plants, climbing lily has leaves, flowers, and a bulb that are poisonous if eaten. ¶ **HOW TO DO IT** ¶ In the spring after the last chance of frost, you can safely plant your climbing lilies. Fill a 15-inch-deep container with thoroughly moist potting mix to within 2 inches of the rim. For each lily, make a hole that is 4 inches deep and add a teaspoon of good-quality timed-release low-nitrogen pelleted plant food to the bottom of the hole. ¶ Place a bulb at the bottom of the hole, fill the hole with potting mix, packing it gently. Pat down the surface of the mix, and water to fill in any air pockets. ¶ Use a 4-foot-tall wire cylinder for the climbing structure. Carefully sink it into the container, spreading out the legs evenly. If the cylinder seems like it may topple, weave three evenly spaced garden stakes through the wire cylinder down into the potting mix. Alternatively, erect a 5-foot-high wire cage that sits on the ground and encircles the container. Measure how much wire you need to completely encompass the container. Cut a piece that size and with wire or string tie the ends together to form a circle. ¶ Guide the stems up the climbing structure until they fasten on by themselves. Keep the mix moist, but not soggy, and fertilize ✐

Climbing Lily
Gloriosa rothschildiana
❧

What You Need
2 bulbs
15-inch-deep container
Potting mix
Timed-release low-nitrogen
pelleted plant food
4-foot-tall wire cylinder or
5-foot-tall wire cage
3 stakes, if necessary
Low-nitrogen liquid fertilizer
formulated for container plants
❧

Hardiness
Tender
❧

Growing Conditions
Light shade
❧

Climbing Method
Tendrils
❧

When to Plant
After the last chance of frost
❧

When to Prune
As necessary to control growth
❧

When Blooms Appear
Summer
❧

every three weeks with a low-nitrogen liquid fertilizer formulated for container plants. ¶ Climbing lilies will keep blooming in the same container for several years. Each year after they bloom, make sure not to cut off the foliage until it has turned brown; the food from the leaves moves to the bulb and is stored there for next year's bloom. Protect the bulbs during the winter by placing the container in a sheltered spot where the temperatures will not fall below 40°F. ¶ Continue to water regularly during the winter, for lily bulbs should never dry out, but do not allow the mix to become soggy or the bulbs will rot.

VINES WITH
AN EDIBLE
HARVEST

The perfect combination of beauty and function is debated among philosophers, artists, architects, and engineers, but gardeners recognize it immediately in luxuriant vines that produce delicious-tasting fruits or vegetables. You can appreciate many vines for their beauty while savoring their bountiful delicacies as well. What more perfect combination of beauty and function could one wish for than the cool, dappled shade of an arbor created by sheltering vines laden with sun-warmed grapes? ❧ Those gardeners with small spaces who want to harvest cucumbers, squash, melons, or pumpkins need only to persuade the supple and pliant vines to climb upward through soft netting or wooden trellises. Beans will twine around a slender strand of string and head for the clouds. Tepees or towers, which add an interesting vertical accent in the garden, will tame far-reaching pumpkin vines. (These are easily put together from rough wood or branches, with strings for cross-ties.) ❧ If your preference is for perennial vines like figs, kiwis, or grapes, look for permanent sites that are large enough for these towering vines and that make use of their deciduous nature. Vines leafing out in summer and shedding their leaves in winter may be the perfect solution for south- or west-facing windows and porches, which call for shade in summer but need every last ray of warm sunshine during winter's cold. ❧ Vines planted underneath the eaves of a house on a south-facing wall will receive some frost protection, so don't despair if you think your climate limits your selection. Explore your garden's microclimates and investigate the hardiest variety of the vine you want to grow. Hybridizers have developed varieties for almost all climate ranges. ❧ You may want to avoid planting vines with edible fruits on arbors with seating, for the dropped fruit can stain furniture and clothing. Remember also when choosing your site that the willowy twig you plant will grow and spread, so plan for its space needs and provide sturdy support. Adding extra support after planting may be difficult and expensive, so planning ahead is judicious.

Espalier fig

Many shrubs and trees have branches as supple as vines and are often treated just like vines. The fig, for example, one of the oldest of humankind's foods, espaliers easily.

Undeterred by this Mediterranean plant's love of warm weather, gardeners in colder climates have trained its pliant stems flat along sun-warmed walls for century upon century. Now there are very cold hardy varieties to choose from, so you can grow figs easily in all but the coldest climates. ¶ To make space for fig trees in your garden, follow the ancient tradition of espaliering them into a long hedge or a garden room divider. In warm-winter climates where they grow to 30 feet, you can train a fig to cover a pergola or a walkway arch. If you live in a cold-winter climate, look for a south-facing house wall with overhanging eaves or train your fig to a trellis in a large container and move it indoors to overwinter in a cool, sheltered spot. ¶ Don't be afraid to prune figs hard, for they grow back easily and without damage. ¶ **HOW TO DO IT** ¶ In the spring after the last chance of frost, you can safely plant your new fig. Before planting, submerge the container in a sink or bucket of water until air bubbles cease to appear. ¶ In prepared garden soil that is thoroughly moist, dig a hole for the plant that is at least twice as wide and twice as deep as the container. To the bottom of the hole add a good-quality timed-release low-nitrogen pelleted plant food, following the directions on the package. ¶ Gently remove the plant and its potting mix from the container, and set it in the hole so that the top of the root ball is just at soil level. Fill the hole with soil, packing it gently around the roots. Pat down the soil surface, and water to fill in any air pockets. Once the weather has warmed the ground, mulch the plant with 3 to 4 inches of organic compost. ✧

Fig
Ficus carica 'Mission', 'Turkey', 'Brown Turkey', or any variety appropriate to your region

What You Need
Container plant
Timed-release low-nitrogen pelleted plant food
Up to 20 feet of wall, fence, or other climbing structure
Plant ties
Organic compost

Hardiness
Some hardy to 0°F, others tender

Growing Conditions
3/4 of a day of direct sun

Climbing Method
None, needs tying

When to Plant
Bare root in spring; container plant from spring to late summer

When to Prune
Hard in winter to shape, lightly after fruiting and throughout the year

When Fruits Appear
In summer and again in fall

¶ In winter, when the plant is dormant, prune it to an espalier shape. First prune out any deadwood, crossing branches, or overly vigorous shoots. Then choose the branches you wish to make your structure and prune out the rest; select two branches on opposite sides of the tree if you want a horizontal hedge, six branches if you want a tall espalier against a wall. Tie the branches to the climbing structure or wall. Prune again lightly after the first harvest of figs to maintain the espalier shape. ¶ Figs will bear fruit in early summer and then again in fall.

White pumpkins

Fancy yourself with a jack-o'-lantern that shimmers ghostly white in the moonlight. French white pumpkins have made their way to America, and seeds are now available from mail-order catalogues. Grow them for their unusual creamy skin tone and richly flavored flesh. ¶ White pumpkins weigh about 10 to 12 pounds and are about a foot across, easy for little folk to carry and to carve. Hide a couple until after Halloween and cook them up for soups and pies. This pumpkin has great flavor. ¶ Pumpkins are generally greedy about garden space, but the size of these white pumpkins makes it a snap to grow them vertically. Create a wooden tepee or tower and train your pumpkin up the sides, or thread the long stems through wire cages or wooden trellises or along walls. ¶ White pumpkins take about one hundred days to produce fruit, so start seeds indoors. After the last chance of frost has passed and the ground has warmed up, set out the plants. ¶ **HOW TO DO IT** ¶ Sow your seeds indoors six to eight weeks before the last expected frost. Soak them for one to three hours, then bury them 1 inch deep in potting mix (as described on p. 23). Seedlings emerge in ten to fourteen days. ¶ After the last chance of frost, you can safely plant the young plants outdoors. Transplant them when they are 4 to 6 inches tall. Make sure to harden them off for a week by leaving them outside in a protected area during the day and bringing them inside at night. Before planting, submerge the transplants in their containers in a sink or bucket of water until air bubbles cease to appear. ¶ In prepared garden soil that is thoroughly moist, make a hill about 12 inches across and 5 inches high. In each hill, make two holes opposite each other and about 4 inches wide and 4 inches deep. Gently remove one plant and its potting mix from the container and set it in one of the holes so that the top of the root ball is just at soil level. Fill the hole with soil, packing it ✐

White Pumpkin
Cucurbita maxima *'Lumina'*
❧

What You Need
Seeds
Containers to start seedlings
Potting mix
Up to 15 feet of wall, trellis,
or other climbing structure
Plant ties, if necessary
Low-nitrogen liquid fertilizer
Organic compost
❧

Hardiness
Tender
❧

Growing Conditions
3/4 of a day of direct sun
❧

Climbing Method
Tendrils
❧

When to Sow
Indoors 6 to 8 weeks before last frost
❧

When to Prune
After choosing 4 or 5 pumpkins to mature,
pick off flowers and other fruits
❧

When Fruits Appear
100 days after sowing
❧

gently around the roots. Place a second plant in the other hole. Pat down the soil surface and water to fill in any air pockets. If you are using a wire cage for support, gently insert it over the hill and two plants. If you are planting a number of hills, be sure to make the rows at least 3 feet apart. ¶ As the pumpkin stems grow, guide them up the climbing structure, weaving them through or tying them loosely to the support. Keep the soil moist but not soggy, and fertilize with a low-nitrogen liquid fertilizer every two weeks. Once the weather has warmed the ground, mulch each plant with 3 to 4 inches of organic compost in a circle 12 inches across. When the pumpkins have grown to the size of a softball, choose the four or five nearest the stem and allow these to mature. Remove the other pumpkins and flowers.

Kiwis

Late in the 1970s, fuzzy little brown-skinned, egg-shaped fruits from New Zealand made a presence in the showiest restaurants. Kiwis had stormed the United States, and soon home gardeners were searching for them in nurseries. ¶ *Kiwis are hardy to Zone 6, but in colder climates, you might consider growing them under glass. As deciduous plants, they can be very useful in a large greenhouse to shade other plants from intense sunlight in summer and yet not restrict light in wintertime. ¶ Kiwi plants require a rich soil, ample water, and regular feeding throughout the summer. These are big growers, so plan to give them space, and since there must be a male and a female plant to produce fruit, you will need at least two plants. Prune them vigorously to increase the fruit.* ¶ **HOW TO DO IT** ¶ In the spring after the last chance of frost, you can safely plant your new kiwi vines. Before planting, submerge the containers in a sink or bucket of water until air bubbles cease to appear. ¶ In prepared garden soil that is thoroughly moist, dig a hole for each plant that is at least twice as wide and twice as deep as the container. To the bottom of the hole, add a small amount of a good-quality timed-release low-nitrogen pelleted plant food, following the directions on the package. ¶ Gently remove each plant and its potting mix from the container, and set it in a hole so that the top of the root ball is just at soil level. Fill the holes with soil, packing it gently around the roots. Pat down the soil surface, and water to fill in any air pockets. ¶ Support the young vines by tying them to the climbing structure. Keep the soil moist but not soggy, and fertilize with a low-nitrogen liquid fertilizer every two weeks through September. Once the weather has warmed the ground, mulch each plant with 3 to 4 inches of organic compost in a circle 12 inches across.

Kiwi
Actinidia chinensis
❧

What You Need
*1 male plant, 1 or more female plants
Timed-release low-nitrogen
pelleted plant food
Up to 30 feet of wall, fence,
or other climbing structure
Plant ties
Low-nitrogen liquid plant food
Organic compost*
❧

Hardiness
Semihardy
❧

Growing Conditions
1/2 day of direct sun
❧

Climbing Method
Twining stems
❧

When to Plant
Spring to late summer
❧

When to Prune
*In winter to cut out old wood, in summer to
shorten new shoots*
❧

When Fruits Appear
Fall
❧

SCARLET RUNNER BEANS

Runner beans are a distinct variety of bean, different from bush beans and pole beans. The major problem in growing them is choosing when and what to eat. The fragrant displays of scarlet, sweet-pea-like blooms are edible, but of course popping the candy-sweet flowers into your mouth for a garden snack or picking them to sprinkle decoratively over soups and salads deprives you of the delicious beans. Pick the beans when they are still baby-small; at 2 to 3 inches they are tasty and tender. If you miss them at that stage, let them develop until they are full grown, for a crop of dried beans often extolled for their fine meaty character. Make sure to buy the improved varieties bred for good eating, because some varieties are bred solely for their bloom. ¶ Even though they are a different type, runner beans grow just like pole beans, and they need climbing structures to ascend. Try the old-fashioned method of fashioning tripods from bamboo or 2-inch wooden stakes and planting two beans at each corner. Or let their exuberant foliage and flowers ramble through fences or trellises, or even pot them up in containers with wire cages for support. ¶ Don't be discouraged if you don't like eating beans; these charming vines are worth growing anyway. They create a rapid screen, and hummingbirds dance in line for a chance to sip the nectar of the flowers. There are new white-blossomed varieties if you prefer. In mild-winter areas, the vines will regrow every spring from their tuberous roots. In cold climates, some gardeners lift the roots in fall and overwinter them like bulbs, but most just treat scarlet runner beans as an annual and sow new seeds every spring when the ground warms up. ¶ **HOW TO DO IT** ¶ Sow seeds directly in the ground after the last chance of frost has passed. Soak them for one day before you plant them. ¶ Bury each seed one inch deep in prepared garden soil that is thoroughly moist. Pat down the soil over the seeds, and water to fill in any air pockets. Seedlings emerge in ten to fourteen days. ¶ Guide the stems to the climbing structure with ties until they fasten ✐

Scarlet Runner Bean
Phaseolus coccineus 'Red Knight',
'Scarlet Emperor', or other
superior variety
❧

What You Need
Seeds
Up to 8 feet of fence, trellis,
or other climbing structure
Plant ties
Low-nitrogen liquid fertilizer
Organic compost
❧

Hardiness
Tender
❧

Growing Conditions
¾ of a day of direct sun
❧

Climbing Method
Tendrils
❧

When to Sow
Spring, after the last chance of frost
❧

When to Prune
Only as necessary to control growth
❧

When Blooms Appear
2 months after sowing
❧

on by themselves. Make sure to twist the stems clockwise; you will break the tops off if you twist counterclockwise. ¶ Keep the soil moist but not soggy, and fertilize every two weeks with a low-nitrogen liquid fertilizer. Once the weather has warmed the ground, mulch each plant with 3 to 4 inches of organic compost in a circle 12 inches across. ¶ For dried beans, leave beans on the vine until they dry out and turn brown. Pick them off and store them in a paper bag in a warm dry place to cure. When the husk feels dry and brittle, separate the seeds from the pods by hand and store the beans in sealed glass jars. Pop the jars into the freezer for three or four days to counter any infestation of bean weevils, little bugs that lay their eggs in the beans while they are still in the garden.

Grapes

Grapes are among the most pleasing vining plants with edible harvests. Since ancient times, they have been cultivated for wine and for the table; twining among the beams of a shady arbor, these remarkable vines are almost as good as having your own backyard supermarket. Brine the early tender leaves to make Greek dolmas, savory bites of rice and meat encased in grape leaves. Enjoy the summer shade the vines provide and in the fall pluck the sweet grapes for eating out of your hand, jellying, or making a syrup with the taste of summer. Prunings can be intertwined to make wreaths or dried and chopped to make smoky-flavored barbecue fuel. A friend sacrifices some of the early little green grapes to add to her flower arrangements. ¶ A few caveats: Choose a variety appropriate to your climate; check with your local nurseries for types that will fruit well in your area. Create a grape arbor to shelter a hot passageway or a sunny window, but remember that when the grapes are at their peak and ready to harvest, winged creatures come to enjoy them, making use of the area temporarily less appealing. Plant several varieties to have grapes all summer long, but not more than you can use. Grapes are very prolific. Be prepared for some pruning when the vines are dormant, and a bit of summer training. Plant bare-root plants, available in late winter, as soon as you can work the ground. ¶ **HOW TO DO IT** ¶ In the spring after the last chance of frost, you can safely plant your new grape vines. Before planting bare-root vines, unwrap the plastic outer covering. Submerge the vines in a sink or bucket of water until air bubbles cease to appear. If you are planting from a container, submerge it in the same way. ¶ In prepared garden soil that is thoroughly moist, dig a hole for each plant that is at least twice as wide and twice as deep as the vine roots or container. Space plants at least 24 inches apart. To the bottom of the planting hole, add a small amount of good-quality timed-release low-nitrogen pelleted plant food, {continues} ➤

Grape
Vitis 'Himrod,' 'Red Flame,' 'Perlette,' or a variety appropriate to your region

What You Need
2 or more bare-root plants
Timed-release low-nitrogen pelleted plant food
Up to 20 feet of wall, fence, or other climbing structure
Plant ties
Low-nitrogen liquid plant food
Organic compost

Hardiness
Hardy varieties available for all but the coldest areas

Growing Conditions
A full day of direct sun

Climbing Method
None, need tying

When to Plant
Bare root in spring, container plant until midsummer

When to Prune
In late winter to shape, lightly in summer to train new growth

When Fruits Appear
Third year after planting, depending upon variety

following the directions on the package. ¶ For bare-root vines, make a pyramid of soil in the bottom of the hole and spread the roots over the pyramid, setting the crown of the plant just at soil level. ¶ For container vines, gently remove the vine and its potting mix from the container, and set it in the hole so that the top of the root ball is just at soil level. Fill the hole with soil, packing it gently around the roots. Pat down the soil surface and water to fill in any air pockets. Prune back the newly planted vine to the first "eye," or bud, almost down to the level of the soil. ¶ Keep the soil moist but not soggy, and fertilize with a low-nitrogen liquid fertilizer every two weeks until September. Once the weather has warmed the ground, mulch each plant with 3 to 4 inches of organic compost in a circle 12 inches across. ¶ The first winter, remove all the growth except a single strong cane. That spring, when shoots begin to grow, choose one leading shoot and guide it up the climbing structure, securing it with ties. Again, prune out all the other shoots. When the vine reaches the top of the climbing structure, pinch out the tip of the shoot. Other shoots will grow, and you should train these as you wish over the climbing structure. ¶ In succeeding winters, cut out the spindly new growth and thin canes. Continue to apply fertilizer every spring to maintain healthy growth. In summer, train new growth to the structure and prune out overvigorous shoots.

VINES FOR
A BURST OF
SEASONAL
COLOR

Gardeners mark the year by the blooming seasons of their favorite plants as much as by the repetitive parade of days and months. What more pleasant record of time than the mad eruption of color that different plants provide month by month throughout the year? Seasonal color makes gardening an anticipatory event, from the first drifts of wisteria to the last garnet-colored leaf on a Virginia creeper. ❧ Planning a garden for bursts of color from spring to fall takes some work with pencil and paper. Exploratory trips to public gardens and nurseries throughout the year will widen your vocabulary of garden plants and their flowering habits. If you are dreaming of a big, smashing block of color, coordinate it with the rest of your garden so that it complements rather than clashes with other plants in bloom at the same time. ❧ The Europeans have long specialized in combining several vining plants in their gardens. Choose the colors you like to see combined and then match plants to your scheme. Drape pink roses and burgundy clematis together along a garden wall. A bright nasturtium will climb up the more somber evergreen jasmine, its blossoms making gem-bright spots of color among the jasmine's dark green leaves. Try a summer-blooming blue clematis with pink, blue, and purple morning glories for a pleasing color harmony. Or intertwine the spring-flowering evergreen clematis with the later-blooming scarlet trumpet vine for a long season of bloom. ❧ Site your vines where you will have the opportunity to enjoy them daily. Their blooms are all too brief, and experiencing them every day through the kitchen window, from your favorite garden bench, or through the front door rewards you with the pleasure every gardener deserves.

HARDENBERGIA

Here is one of spring's heralds. Just when you think winter will never end, hardenbergia bursts into bloom as a signal of sweet spring's imminent arrival. The evergreen leaves are slender and graceful all year long, but the real show is in the bloom. Varieties in sweet-pea colors of purple, pink, and white make blankets of color draped over walls or small trellises. Plant all three colors for a rainbow mingling. ¶ Hardenbergia is a small vine, manageable in little gardens. It will not reach more than 10 feet in height, so use it for an effective low screen. It is also perfect for training over low fences or up front porch banisters. ¶ This is a tender vine; it doesn't like the temperature dropping below 24°F. In cold-winter areas, grow it beneath a south-facing overhang for protection from the cold and mulch the roots with 1 to 2 feet of compost. ¶ **HOW TO DO IT** ¶ In the spring after the last chance of frost, you can safely plant your new hardenbergia vine. Before planting, submerge the container in a sink or bucket of water until air bubbles cease to appear. ¶ In prepared garden soil that is thoroughly moist, dig a hole for the plant that is at least twice as wide and twice as deep as the container. To the bottom of the hole, add a small amount of good-quality timed-release low-nitrogen plant food, following the directions on the package. ¶ Gently remove the plant and its potting mix from the container, and set it in the hole so that the top of the root ball is just at soil level. Fill the hole with soil, packing it gently around the roots. Pat down the soil surface and water to fill in any air pockets. ¶ Guide the plant to the climbing structure with ties until it fastens on by itself. Hardenbergia does not like to be overwatered so keep the soil moist but not soggy. Once the weather has warmed the ground, mulch your plant with 3 to 4 inches of organic compost in a circle 12 inches across. Fertilize with a low-nitrogen liquid fertilizer in midsummer.

Hardenbergia
Hardenbergia violacea

❧

What You Need
Container plant
Timed-release low-nitrogen
pelleted plant food
Up to 10 feet of wall, fence,
or other climbing structure
Plant ties
Low-nitrogen liquid fertilizer
Organic compost

❧

Hardiness
Tender

❧

Growing Conditions
1/2 day of direct sun

❧

Climbing Method
Twining stems

❧

When to Plant
Spring to late summer

❧

When to Prune
After blooming in spring and as
necessary to control growth

❧

When Blooms Appear
Late winter to early spring

❧

WISTERIA

Flowers by nature are transitory, but artists have often captured their effect in paintings and drawings. Seventeenth-century Japanese prints show kimono-clad maidens beneath the drooping blooms of wisteria. Long before plant collectors brought this vine to Europe and the United States, the pealike blooms of the wisteria were treasured in Asian gardens and recorded in Asian art. ¶ Wisteria was also popular as an art subject during the American art deco period of the early 1900s, most spectacularly in the stained-glass windows and lamps of the Tiffany glassworks. While we can't all afford a Tiffany, we can gain pleasure from planting and growing the real thing. ¶ Wisteria is at its best when trained along arcades or arbors. It shows a different form in every season: Winter reveals its twining gray sculptural branches; spring brings fragrance and blossom followed by filmy foliage. In summer, the leaves throw lacy shadows, and later in the season furry seedpods develop. In fall, the leaves turn bright yellow. ¶ There are both Chinese and Japanese varieties, but choose the Chinese wisteria for the very beautiful bloom shape, rounder and fuller than the Japanese type. The blooms of Chinese wisteria burst from their buds on bare stems all at once for full effect; the Japanese wisteria blooms unfurl more slowly among the young foilage. ¶ Be sure to plan room for wisteria to grow. This long-lived vine loves to spread, and as it matures, it becomes very large and heavy. It will topple over or pull down anything but a very sturdy support. ¶ **HOW TO DO IT** ¶ In the spring after the last chance of frost, you can safely plant your new vine. Before planting, submerge the container in a sink or bucket of water until air bubbles cease to appear. ¶ In prepared garden soil that is thoroughly moist, dig a hole for the plant that is at least twice as wide and twice as deep as the container. To the bottom of the hole, add a small amount of a good-quality timed-release high-nitrogen pelleted plant food, following the directions on the package. ¶ Gently remove the plant and its potting mix from the container, and set it in the hole so that the top of ✒

Wisteria

Wisteria sinensis 'Alba' (white bloom),
'Black Dragon', or 'Prolific'

❧

What You Need
Container plant
Timed-release high-nitrogen
pelleted plant food
At least 30 feet of sturdy support
Plant ties
Organic compost

❧

Hardiness
Hardy

❧

Growing Conditions
3/4 to a full day of direct sun

❧

Climbing Method
Twining stems

❧

When to Plant
Spring to midsummer

❧

When to Prune
In winter and again in summer
to thin out growth

❧

When Blooms Appear
Late spring, sometimes repeating in summer

❧

the root ball is just at soil level. Fill the hole with soil, packing it gently around the roots. Pat down the soil surface and water to fill in any air pockets. ¶ Guide the stems to the climbing structure with ties until they fasten on by themselves. Keep the soil moist but not soggy. Once the weather has warmed the ground, mulch the plant with 3 to 4 inches of organic compost in a circle 12 inches across. In summer, fertilize the young plants with a once-a-year application of timed-release high-nitrogen pelleted plant food. ¶ Prune your plant to establish the main stems. Every winter, thin back side shoots to create the shape you wish. After it blooms, cut back the long shoots to maintain the vine's shape. Expect plants to bloom after three years. If a mature plant fails to blossom, cut back on the nitrogen fertilizer for a year.

CLEMATIS AND ROSES TOGETHER

Lately, gardeners traveling to Europe have discovered the shocking and at second glance pleasing sight of several vines mingling. ¶ Intertwining vines adds the aesthetic complexity of a sonata while conveniently allowing you to piggyback two plants and save space in a small garden. ¶ Clematis and roses are a classic pairing. Use an established climbing rose to provide the support structure, for the clematis will climb 5 to 7 feet its first season in the garden. The two plants should bloom at the same time. Plant the clematis a good foot away from the base of the rose so the roots will not compete. Clematis, like lilies, prefer their roots to be partially shaded, so make sure to mulch your plant generously or plant it behind a small shrub or ground cover. Combine 'Iceberg' with Clematis montana 'Rubra', for a white with pink, and 'Queen Elizabeth' with Clematis montana 'Rubra', for a pink on pink. ¶ **HOW TO DO IT** ¶ In the spring after the last chance of frost, you can safely plant your new clematis vine. Before planting, submerge the container in a sink or bucket of water until air bubbles cease to appear. ¶ At least 1 foot away from the rose, in prepared garden soil that is thoroughly moist, dig a hole for the clematis that is at least twice as wide and twice as deep as the container. To the bottom of the hole, add a small amount of a good-quality timed-release low-nitrogen pelleted plant food, following the directions on the package. ¶ Gently remove the clematis and its potting mix from the container, and set it in the hole so that the top of the root ball is just at soil level. Fill the hole with soil, packing it gently around the roots. Pat down the surface and water to fill in any air pockets. ¶ As the stems grow guide them into the rose branches. Keep the soil moist but not soggy. Once the weather has warmed the ground, mulch the clematis with 4 to 6 inches of organic compost in a circle 12 inches across. Fertilize with a low-nitrogen liquid fertilizer once a month until September.

Clematis
Clematis montana 'Rubra'

❧

What You Need
Container plant
Timed-release low-nitrogen pelleted plant food
Climbing rose up to 10 feet tall
Organic compost
Low-nitrogen liquid fertilizer

❧

Hardiness
Hardy

❧

Growing Conditions
$1/2$ day of direct sun

❧

Climbing Method
Twining stems

❧

When to Plant
Spring

❧

When to Prune
As necessary to control growth

❧

When Blooms Appear
Spring

❧

CLIMBING HYDRANGEA

This regal hydrangea spreads over walls and up the sides of buildings in a stately and elegant fashion. A true climber, its branches have aerial roots, like ivy, that grip and allow the plant to scale even the flattest surfaces. Unlike some vines, it finds rock, stone, concrete, and stucco easy to ascend. It's also unusual in preferring north-facing or partially shady westerly aspects. By gently guiding the branches and pinning them down temporarily until they catch hold, you can create a tracery on your walls up to 50 feet high. ¶ Like the other hydrangeas, this plant loses its leaves in the fall, but the design of its bare branches against a wall adds an elegance to the winter season. In the spring and early summer, it produces large white flattish flower heads that polka-dot the branches. For the first couple of seasons, the growth may be slow; but don't worry, once established it will reward you with many years of glorious bloom and foliage. ¶ **HOW TO DO IT** ¶ In the spring after the last chance of frost, you can safely plant your new vine. Before planting, submerge the container in a sink or bucket of water until air bubbles cease to appear. ¶ In prepared garden soil that is thoroughly moist, dig a hole for the plant that is at least twice as wide and twice as deep as the container. To the bottom of the hole, add a small amount of a good-quality timed-release low-nitrogen pelleted plant food, following the directions on the package. ¶ Gently remove the plant and its potting mix from the container, and set it in the hole so that the top of the root ball is just at soil level. Fill the hole with soil, packing it gently around the roots. Pat down the surface and water to fill in any air pockets. ¶ Guide the stems to the climbing structure with ties until they fasten on by themselves. Keep the soil moist but not soggy, and fertilize with a timed-release low-nitrogen pelleted plant food in midsummer. Once the weather has warmed the ground, mulch the plant with 3 to 4 inches of organic compost in a circle 12 inches across.

Climbing Hydrangea
Hydrangea anomala *subsp.*
petiolaris; Schizophragma
hydrangeoides

❧

What You Need
Container plant
Timed-release low-nitrogen
pelleted plant food
Up to 30 feet of wall, fence,
or other climbing structure
Plant ties
Organic compost

❧

Hardiness
Hardy

❧

Growing Conditions
1/2 day of direct sun

❧

Climbing Method
Clinging roots on stems

❧

When to Plant
Spring to late summer

❧

When to Prune
As necessary to control growth

❧

When Blooms Appear
Summer

❧

CLIMBING ICEBERG ROSE

Every garden should have a prima donna, a plant that has presence and stands out as the star. 'Iceberg' in bloom fits the bill; in the gloaming of early evening, the luminescent white flowers are as showy as a mass of exploding fireworks. Plant a climbing 'Iceberg' and you will have a star that performs reliably without persnickety requirements. ¶ Rosarians have long known and highly rated 'Iceberg', but until recently it was not available in a climbing form. Leave it unpruned for the first two years so you can get an idea of its shape. The third year prune it to the shape you wish. ¶ **HOW TO DO IT** ¶ In the spring after the last chance of frost, you can safely plant your new rose. Before planting, submerge the container in a sink or bucket of water until air bubbles cease to appear. ¶ In prepared garden soil that is thoroughly moist, dig a hole for the plant that is at least twice as wide and twice as deep as the container. To the bottom of the hole, add a small amount of a good-quality pelleted plant food formulated for roses, following the directions on the package. ¶ Gently remove the rose and its potting mix from the container, and set it in the hole so that the top of the root ball is just at soil level. Fill the hole with soil, packing it gently around the roots. Pat down the soil surface and water to fill in any air pockets. If you are planting a bare-root rose, see p. 24. ¶ Guide the canes to the climbing structure with ties. Keep the soil moist but not soggy. Fertilize the rose every month with a good-quality pelleted plant food formulated for roses, following the directions on the package. ¶ The third winter, begin to prune your 'Iceberg'. Cut out canes that cross into the center and also the stems less than ½ inch in diameter. Remove side shoots to create the shape you wish. Every year after the rose blooms, trim off the spent flowers and cut back the long canes to maintain its shape.

Climbing 'Iceberg'
Rosa 'Iceberg'

What You Need
Bare-root or container plant
Pelleted plant food formulated for roses
At least 15 feet of wall, fence,
or other climbing structure
Plant ties

Hardiness
Hardy

Growing Conditions
³/₄ to a full day of direct sun

Climbing Method
None, needs tying

When to Plant
Bare root in spring as early as the ground
can be worked; container plant
from spring to midsummer

When to Prune
In winter, and again in summer to
cut off bloom and thin canes

When Blooms Appear
Late spring, repeating in summer

VIRGINIA CREEPER

Seasonal color can come from more than glamorous blooms in spring or summer. During its growing season, gardeners appreciate Virginia creeper for its pretty five-fingered, leafy green cover and bright purple-blue berries, rather than for its quite inconspicuous flowers. However, it is the fall they wait for in breath-holding anticipation. As the nights turn cold, Virginia creeper's autumn cloak paints sides of buildings brilliant ruby and garnet colors. ¶ This vine climbs by mighty sucker disks; an unpainted wall or concrete or stucco building is ideal. You may not want to use it on wood paneling or shingles. ¶ Virginia creeper is very tolerant of sun or shade, but it does appreciate water and a little fertilizer in spring and then again in midsummer. Remember that Virginia creeper sheds its leaves in winter, so don't use it as a privacy screen. However, the bare limbs make an exquisitely delicate pattern. ¶ **HOW TO DO IT** ¶ In the spring after the last chance of frost, you can safely plant your new vine. Before planting, submerge the container in a sink or bucket of water until air bubbles cease to appear. ¶ In prepared garden soil that is thoroughly moist, dig a hole for the plant that is at least twice as wide and twice as deep as the container. To the bottom of the hole, add a small amount of a good-quality timed-release low-nitrogen pelleted plant food, following the directions on the package. ¶ Gently remove the plant and its potting mix from the container, and set it in the hole so that the top of the root ball is just at soil level. Fill the hole with soil, packing it gently around the roots. Pat down the soil surface and water to fill in any air pockets. ¶ Guide the stems to the climbing structure with ties until they fasten on by themselves. Keep the soil moist but not soggy, and fertilize with a low-nitrogen pelleted plant food in spring and again in midsummer. Once the weather has warmed the ground, mulch your vine with 3 to 4 inches of organic compost in a circle 12 inches across.

Virginia Creeper
Parthenocissus quinquefolia
❧

What You Need
Container plant
Timed-release low-nitrogen
pelleted plant food
Up to 50 feet of wall, fence,
or other climbing structure
Plant ties
Organic compost
❧

Hardiness
Hardy
❧

Growing Conditions
1/2 day of direct sun
❧

Climbing Method
Suction disks on stems
❧

When to Plant
Spring to late summer
❧

When to Prune
As necessary to control growth
❧

When Blooms Appear
Summer, brilliantly colored leaves in fall
❧

VINES TO
QUICKLY
COVER A
FENCE OR
WALL

Some vines leap out of the ground ready to climb anything in sight—they hit the ground climbing. These troopers cover unseemly objects, provide privacy and screening, and blast a spot of color into your garden quicker than quick. ❧ Annual vines get off to the fastest start. Seeds sown directly into prepared garden soil produce in a matter of months prodigious vines that grow and grow and grow. Some of the annual vines stay small, which makes them useful for low fences and small trellises. The annual vines in this book have color, many also have fragrance, and some, like the black-eyed Susans and morning glories, self-sow, returning unaided year after year. ❧ Have patience with the slightly slower perennial vines. They may take a bit longer to establish, but they will be with you for many years. You can depend upon their bloom and foliage, which is especially useful if you need a permanent screen for privacy in a location too narrow for a hedge or you want to cover an ugly structure you can't remove. ❧ Some perennials die back when fall weather becomes frosty, which can be an advantage. Grown over a window or a porch, for example, vines such as clematis provide a leafy summer screen from intense heat then, when they lose their leaves, the winter sun can shine in. Deciduous vines also provide a temporary change of gardenscape. Come springtime, you can be confident that they will reemerge, ready to cover, blossom, and perfume once again. ❧ Measure the amount of area you wish to cover with your vine. Perhaps you want to throw up temporary greenery while a tree or shrub becomes established, or you need to disguise the tool shed. Choose the vine that fits the space so you achieve your goal and are not faced with heavy pruning or bare, ugly spots the vine doesn't reach.

OLD-FASHIONED PASSION FLOWER

The passion flower has a very unusual shape. Supposedly, the missionaries who came across it in Central and South America saw a Christian motif in its flower parts. Looking at the flower, it is a curious reconstruction, and young children are equally as apt to see a dinosaur face in its frilly center. ¶ This is a very vigorous evergreen climber, which although tender and likely to suffer dieback after frosts, will make it through cold winters. Its tendrils attach swiftly to fences and trellises, and the large white flowers appear throughout the summer. The glossy foliage prefers sun to make its flowers open, but it will accept some shade. ¶ In warm areas, edible fruit will follow the flowers. Australians cook up the fruits with sugar to make a thick syrup, which they team with sparkling soda for a refreshing summer drink. ¶ **HOW TO DO IT** ¶ In the spring after the last chance of frost, you can safely plant your new vine. Before planting, submerge the container in a sink or bucket of water until air bubbles cease to appear. ¶ In prepared garden soil that is thoroughly moist, dig a hole for the plant that is at least twice as wide and twice as deep as the container. To the bottom of the hole, add a small amount of a good-quality timed-release low-nitrogen pelleted plant food, following the directions on the package. ¶ Gently remove the plant and its potting mix from the container, and set it in the hole so that the top of the root ball is just at soil level. Fill the hole with soil, packing it gently around the roots. Pat down the soil surface and water to fill in any air pockets. ¶ Guide the stems to the climbing structure with ties until they fasten on by themselves. Keep the soil moist but not soggy, and fertilize with a low-nitrogen liquid fertilizer once a month until September. ¶ Prune your vine lightly to shape it. Leave the spent blossoms on the vine so that it can produce fruit.

Old-Fashioned Passion Flower
Passiflora caerulea

❧

What You Need
Container plant
Timed-release low-nitrogen
pelleted plant food
Up to 8 feet of wall, fence,
or other climbing structure
Plant ties
Low-nitrogen liquid fertilizer

❧

Hardiness
Tender stems, but will regrow from roots

❧

Growing Conditions
1/2 day of direct sun

❧

Climbing Method
Tendrils

❧

When to Plant
Spring

❧

When to Prune
Lightly throughout the year, to shape

❧

When Blooms Appear
Spring to summer

❧

Hop

A "hop, skip, and a jump" describes the way the vine grows, scurrying up walls, leaping over sheds, covering in a tidy green leafy blanket anything you put in front of it. The flowers are not spectacular, something like a soft pinecone in a delicate shade of lime green (and smelling piny as well). ¶ There are annual and perennial hop vines; the annual is grown from seeds, the perennial from roots. Although it may be difficult to find, plant a perennial vine. In the fall, when temperatures start to get nippy, the vine will turn brown. Cut it back to the ground and wait for its return in spring. ¶ For the record, it's the pollen of hops that adds body and flavor to beer. ¶ **HOW TO DO IT** ¶ In the spring after the last chance of frost, you can safely plant your new vine. Before planting, submerge the roots in a sink or bucket of water for one hour. ¶ In prepared garden soil that is thoroughly moist, dig a hole for the vine that is at least 12 inches wide and 12 inches deep. To the bottom of the hole, add a small amount of a good-quality timed-release low-nitrogen pelleted plant food, following the directions on the package. ¶ Gently set the plant in the hole with the thick end up. Make sure the top is just below the soil surface. Fill the hole with soil mixed with compost, packing it gently around the roots. Pat down the soil surface and water to fill in any air pockets. ¶ Keep the soil moist but not soggy, and fertilize with a high-nitrogen liquid fertilizer every two weeks for two months. Once the weather has warmed the ground, mulch each plant with 3 to 4 inches of organic compost in a circle 12 inches across. ¶ As the shoots appear, guide them to the support with ties until they fasten on by themselves. Spread them out in a pattern to cover the surface as you wish. Continue to water regularly. At the end of the growing season, when cool temperatures kill the leaves, cut the stems to the ground. New shoots will emerge in spring.

Hop
Humulus lupulus

❧

What You Need
Perennial hop root
Timed-release low-nitrogen
pelleted plant food
Organic compost
Up to 25 feet of wall, fence,
or other climbing structure
Plant ties
High-nitrogen liquid fertilizer

❧

Hardiness
Hardy

❧

Growing Conditions
¹/₂ day of direct sun

❧

Climbing Method
Twining stems

❧

When to Plant
Early spring

❧

When to Prune
As necessary to control growth;
to the ground in fall

❧

When Blooms Appear
Summer

❧

Scarlet Trumpet Vine

Many garden books draw attention to scarlet trumpet vine's "rampant" growth, and when you witness its enthusiastic clambering over walls and fences, you will surely agree. Although too tender for the snow belt, this vine is a good problem solver for mild-winter gardens requiring a fast-growing, evergreen blanket to erase undesirable features or to provide year-round privacy. Its handsome leaves are only part of its charm, for all summer long, trumpet-shaped bright orange-red flowers bloom with abandon. The young plant may take several months to get established; during that time feed it every two weeks with a high-nitrogen liquid fertilizer and water regularly. Once established, your scarlet trumpet vine will race away and need little water or fertilizer. ¶ Because the nursery trade has recently renamed members of the family, make sure you take home Distictis, not any of the scarlet trumpet vines in the Bignonia family.
¶ **HOW TO DO IT** ¶ In the spring after the last chance of frost, you can safely plant your new vine. Before planting, submerge the container in a sink or bucket of water until air bubbles cease to appear. ¶ In prepared garden soil that is thoroughly moist, dig a hole for the plant that is at least twice as wide and twice as deep as the container. To the bottom of the hole, add a small amount of a good-quality timed-release low-nitrogen pelleted plant food, following the directions on the package. ¶ Gently remove the plant and its potting mix from the container, and set it in the hole so that the root ball is just at soil level. Fill the hole with soil, packing it gently around the roots. Pat down the soil surface and water to fill in any air pockets. ¶ Guide the stems to the climbing structure with ties until they fasten on by themselves. Keep the soil moist but not soggy, and fertilize with a high-nitrogen liquid fertilizer every two weeks for the first two months. Once the weather has warmed the ground, mulch the plant with 3 to 4 inches of organic compost in a circle 12 inches across.

Scarlet Trumpet Vine
Distictis buccinatoria

❧

What You Need
Container plant
Timed-release low-nitrogen
pelleted plant food
Up to 20 feet of wall, fence,
or other climbing structure
Plant ties
High-nitrogen liquid fertilizer
Organic compost

❧

Hardiness
Tender stems, but will usually
regrow from roots

❧

Growing Conditions
1/2 day of direct sun

❧

When to Plant
From spring to late summer

❧

When to Prune
Lightly in spring to shape, after summer
bloom to control growth

❧

When Blooms Appear
July to September

❧

LOOFAHS

The loofah sponges you see for sale in chic gift and bath shops start life as simple gourds. Grow them yourself for the charm of having a homegrown supply of bath and bottle scrubbers. The cheery visage of their bright yellow flowers and the culinary pleasure of their fruits, tasty as any squash when young and tender, add to their merit. Watch them skim up a west-facing trellis, their large leaves providing shade for you from the afternoon sun. ¶ Seeds of these gourds are available, but not widely. (Check the seed sources list on p. 104.) Because loofahs like a long growing season, start the seeds inside and plant the young plants outside when the ground has warmed up, just as you would tomatoes. Dig plenty of high-nitrogen timed-release pelleted plant food and compost into the planting hole before planting. When the weather warms, these plants take off, sometimes covering 20 to 30 feet. Eat the little fruits when they are 2 to 3 inches long. Immerse the mature gourds in water until you can rub off the outer flesh. Let the sponges dry on raised screens, turning them regularly. As they dry, the seeds will break loose and can be shaken out. ¶ **HOW TO DO IT** ¶ Sow your seeds indoors six to eight weeks before the last expected frost. Soak them for one to three hours, then bury them 1 inch deep in potting mix (as described on p. 23). Seedlings emerge in ten to fourteen days. ¶ When night temperatures are above 50°F, you can safely plant the vines outside. Transplant them when they are 4 to 6 inches tall. Make sure to harden them off for a week by leaving them outside in a protected area during the day and bringing them inside at night. Before planting, submerge the transplants in their containers in a sink or bucket of water until air bubbles cease to appear. ¶ In prepared garden soil that is thoroughly moist, dig a hole for each young plant that is at least twice as wide and twice as deep as the container. To the bottom of the hole, add a small amount of a good-quality ✐

Loofah
Luffa aegyptiaca or *L. cylindrica*
❧

What You Need
Seeds
Containers to start seedlings
Potting mix
Timed-release high-nitrogen pelleted plant food
Organic compost
Up to 20 feet of wall, fence, or other climbing structure
Plant ties
High-nitrogen liquid fertilizer
❧

Hardiness
Tender
❧

Growing Conditions
³/₄ to a full day of direct sun
❧

Climbing Method
Tendrils
❧

When to Sow
Indoors 6 to 8 weeks before last frost
❧

When to Prune
As necessary to control growth
❧

When Blooms Appear
Midsummer
❧

timed-release high-nitrogen pelleted plant food, following the directions on the package. Space plants 18 to 24 inches apart. ¶ Gently remove a plant and its potting mix from the container, and set it in the hole so that the top of the root ball is just at soil level. Fill the hole with a mixture of organic compost and soil, packing it gently around the roots. Pat down the surface and water to fill in any air pockets. ¶ Guide the stems to the climbing structure with ties until they fasten on by themselves. Keep the soil moist but not soggy, and fertilize with a high-nitrogen liquid fertilizer every two weeks for two months. Once the weather has warmed the ground, mulch each plant with 3 to 4 inches of organic compost in a circle 12 inches across. ¶ If you want particularly large loofahs, remove some of the first small fruits, limiting the total number on the vine to about six.

HALL'S HONEYSUCKLE

Some of the most important plants in the garden are not luminaries, not wildly bloom-crazy, not inordinately fruitful. They are the steadily reliable ones, vigorous but well-mannered, perfectly suited for the role of the chorus. ¶ Hall's honeysuckle is just such an unassuming plant. It is very vigorous, fast growing, evergreen or semievergreen depending upon winter cold, and covered with fragrant creamy white flowers all summer. Although you may look askance at its tendency to emulate kudzu, because it takes off running, it is more manageable than those wilder varieties of honeysuckle that gardeners chase after with their pruning shears. But do keep thinning out the older stems. Left unpruned, the vine suffers dieback in the center because of lack of light. ¶ Hall's solves tough garden problems. Have a wall you want blanketed with green? Hall's will do it. It's an excellent groundcover, too. If you need to control erosion on a steep bank, Hall's will cement the slope together while presenting a very pleasing aspect. ¶ **HOW TO DO IT** ¶ In the spring after the last chance of frost, you can safely plant your new vine. Before planting, submerge the container in a sink or bucket of water until air bubbles cease to appear. ¶ In prepared garden soil that is thoroughly moist, dig a hole that is at least twice as wide and twice as deep as the container. To the bottom of the hole, add a small amount of a good-quality timed-release low-nitrogen pelleted plant food, following the directions on the package. ¶ Gently remove the plant and its potting mix from the container, and set it in the hole so that the root ball is just at soil level. Fill the hole with soil, packing it gently around the roots. Pat down the soil surface and water to fill in any air pockets. Guide the stems to the climbing structure with ties until they fasten on by themselves. Keep the soil moist but not soggy. Once the weather has warmed the ground, mulch the vine with 3 to 4 inches of organic compost in a circle 12 inches across.

Hall's Honeysuckle
Lonicera japonica 'Halliana'

What You Need
Container plant
Timed-release low-nitrogen
pelleted plant food
Up to 15 feet of wall, fence,
or other climbing structure
Plant ties
Organic compost

Hardiness
Hardy

Growing Conditions
1/2 day of direct sun

Climbing Method
Twining stems

When to Plant
Spring to summer

When to Prune
Severely once a year, lightly in summer
to keep an open framework

When Blooms Appear
Late spring to summer

FRAGRANT

VINES

A lthough not a particularly dictatorial person, I could lay down the law that every garden must have a fragrant plant—in fact, at least one for each season to beckon you out among your flower beds. The sensuous surprise of air awash in scent is part of the mystery and magic of gardening. Of course, for plants, it is a practical matter; fragrance is a siren call to insects and birds, promising nectar or pollen. Tracking the creatures in, as surely as planes to a runway, scent ensures the pollination of the flowers and the continuation of the plant's lifecycle. ❧ Aromatherapy is all the rage in the stores, but you can have it every day without leaving your garden. A pergola clothed in vines offers a natural wraparound fragrance, the blooms sending out a heady perfume to relax you. A vigorous vine will carry fragrance into a second-story bedroom; a nighttime-blooming one will perfume the evening air and make sitting still and quiet in the garden a better night out than dining in a noisy restaurant. ❧ The fragrance of a silky soft blossom is an elemental enjoyment, something that is never the same out of a bottle. Place fragrant vines near doorways, so you pass through a tunnel of sweet scent coming and going. If you have a favorite garden bench, surround it with a fragrant vine, or even two different ones so that you can enjoy the scent all summer long. Instead of those plastic scent cards, use sprays of sweet fresh flowers, their stems wrapped in moist paper towel and sealed with plastic. If you place one in a shady spot in your car, traffic jams somehow won't bother you as much as before.

Rugosa rose

Gardeners adding the scent and beauty of roses to their gardens join a long line of fervent disciples fascinated with this family of flowers. Around 500 B.C. Confucius was describing how to grow roses; a hundred or so years earlier, Sappho had written poems to roses and Greek frescoes already existed that depicted European gardens full of roses. The Virgin Mary supposedly made the first rosary from rolled rose petals as a tribute to Saint Dominic. Since medieval times, various cultures have cooked with rose petals, used distilled rose oil for orgies, and spread roses before kings, queens, and brides. Nowadays, roses chaperone first dates, congratulate marriages and babies, and, of course, preside at gravesides in memory and eternal love. ¶ A "rose is a rose is a rose," but only for novices; rose gardeners know there are many different types of roses. Rugosas are the tough and hardy ones. Disdain the fickle long-stemmed beauties you need to fuss and worry about and grow these disease-resistant, drought-resistant, salt-resistant, sturdy plants. Grow them stretching up against a back fence or as a tall, impenetrable hedge. Because the flowers bloom on old and new wood, rugosas only need pruning to keep them shapely. They are thorny and prickly, but they will reward you with flowers and scent all summer long, and then a crop of scarlet rose hips (the seedpods), which make a soothing, vitamin C-packed rose hip tea. ¶ **HOW TO DO IT** ¶ In the spring after the last chance of frost, you can safely plant your new rose. Before planting, submerge the container in a sink or bucket of water until air bubbles cease to appear. ¶ In prepared garden soil that is thoroughly moist, dig a hole for the plant that is at least twice as wide and twice as deep as the container. To the bottom of the hole, add a small amount of a good-quality pelleted rose food, following the directions on the package. ¶ Gently remove the rose and its potting mix from the container, and set it in the hole so that the top of the root ball is just at soil level. Fill the hole with ✒

Rugosa Rose
Rosa rugosa 'Blanc Double de Coubert', 'Frau Dagmar Hastrup', or 'Will Alderman'

❧

What You Need
Bare-root or container plant
Pelleted plant food formulated for roses
Up to 8 feet of wall, fence, or other climbing structure
Plant ties
Organic compost

❧

Hardiness
Hardy

❧

Growing Conditions
$1/2$ day of direct sun

❧

Climbing Method
None, needs tying

❧

When to Plant
Bare root in spring as early as the ground can be worked; container plants until summer

❧

When to Prune
As necessary to control growth; leave flowers to develop into rose hips

❧

When Blooms Appear
Summer to fall

❧

soil, packing it gently around the roots. Pat down the soil surface and water to fill in any air pockets. If you are planting a bare-root rose, see p. 24. ¶ Guide the canes to the climbing structure with ties. Keep the soil moist but not soggy. Once the weather has warmed the ground, mulch the rose with 3 to 4 inches of organic compost in a circle 12 inches across. Fertilize the rose with monthly applications of pelleted rose plant food, following the directions on the package. ¶ The third winter, begin to prune your rugosa. If you want an open form, cut out canes that cross into the center and also stems less than $1/2$ inch in diameter. For a dense hedge, thin or remove side shoots to create the shape you wish. In summer, leave the spent flowers on the stems to allow rose hips to develop.

EVERGREEN CLEMATIS

If you need a thick perennial covering for a sunny wall or to create a private space, look to the evergreen clematis. The springtime rush of 2- to 3-inch white blooms is perfumed like vanilla and spreads like a foamy wave along the top of the vine. ¶ Evergreen clematis can be slow to get established but once it does, growth will surge along garden walls. If you prefer a pale pink-flowered variety, look for 'Hendersoni Rubra'. ¶ After the spring bloom comes the task of pruning the gangly new growth. If you shirk this job, the center will become bare of leaves. ¶ **HOW TO DO IT** ¶ In the spring after the last chance of frost, you can safely plant your new vine. Before planting, submerge the container in a sink or bucket of water until air bubbles cease to appear. ¶ In prepared garden soil that is thoroughly moist, dig a hole for the plant that is at least twice as wide and twice as deep as the container. To the bottom of the hole, add a small amount of a good-quality timed-release low-nitrogen pelleted plant food, following the directions on the package. ¶ Gently remove the plant and its potting mix from the container, and set it in the hole so that the top of the root ball is just at soil level. Fill the hole with soil, packing it gently around the roots. Pat down the soil surface and water to fill in any air pockets. ¶ Guide the stems to the climbing structure with ties until they fasten on by themselves. Keep the soil moist but not soggy, and fertilize with a low-nitrogen liquid fertilizer every two weeks for the first two months. Once the weather has warmed the ground, mulch the plant with 3 to 4 inches of organic compost in a circle 12 inches across. ¶ Prune vigorously after the plant blooms, trimming back the new growth so that all the remaining stems are exposed to sunlight and the plant will not become tangled and unsightly. Continue to prune lightly throughout the summer to maintain an open structure.

Evergreen Clematis

Clematis armandii

❧

What You Need
Container plant
Timed-release low-nitrogen pelleted plant food
Up to 20 feet of wall, fence, or other climbing structure
Plant ties
Low-nitrogen liquid fertilizer
Organic compost

❧

Hardiness
Hardy to 32°F

❧

Growing Conditions
$1/2$ day of direct sun

❧

Climbing Method
Twining stems

❧

When to Plant
From spring to midsummer

❧

When to Prune
Heavily after spring bloom, then lightly through summer

❧

When Blooms Appear
Early spring

❧

Fragrant rhododendron

Fragrant rhododendron has an open, leggy growing habit, perfect for espaliering. With gentle tutoring, you can shape this evergreen, luxuriant rhody to climb up a trellis, or even to hang over a wall. Position it next to a main walkway so you have a hundred reasons to walk by the richly fragrant, pinky white, bell-like blooms in April or May. ¶ Rhododendrons have slightly fickle requirements, but with a bit of attention will bring beauty to your garden for many years. They prefer dappled shade under tall trees, but in a cool climate, they will tolerate some direct sun. When you plant them, dig lots of organic material into the planting hole and check that the soil drains easily by adding water to the hole and watching how long it takes to empty. If the water takes an hour or more to drain or doesn't drain, then you must dig deeper and add more organic matter so the plant roots will not rot in boggy soil. ¶ Add some acid fertilizer to the planting hole, and after you have planted the rhododendron, make a generous mulch over the surface with pine needles, oak leaves, or wood products, to keep the soil acid. Lastly, never cultivate under your rhododendron, because the feeder roots grow at the surface and you will destroy them. Keep watering during hot and dry times; the plants do not like to dry out. ¶ **HOW TO DO IT** ¶ In the spring after the last chance of frost, you can safely plant your new rhododendron. Before planting, submerge the container in a sink or bucket of water until air bubbles cease to appear. ¶ In prepared garden soil that is thoroughly moist, dig a hole for the plant that is at least twice as wide and twice as deep as the container. To the bottom of the hole, add a small amount of a timed-release acid plant food, following the directions on the package. ¶ Gently remove the plant and its potting mix from the container, and set it in the hole so that the root ball is just about 1 inch above the surrounding soil level. Fill the hole with a mixture of 50 percent soil and 50 percent organic compost, packing it ✐

gently around the roots. Pat down the soil surface and water to fill in any air pockets. Spread a mulch 3 inches deep of pine needles, oak leaves, or wood products around the base of the plant. ¶ Guide the stems to the climbing structure with ties, spreading the stems to form the desired shape. Keep the soil moist but not soggy, and fertilize with a timed-release acid plant food when growth begins in spring and then again around bloom time. Continue to feed monthly until August. ¶ After bloom, gently break off the spent flowers, being careful not to damage the new growth showing green just beneath them. Continue to train the stems in the shape you wish. Prune crossing or undesired branches back to the main stem.

Moonflower

The Victorians trained moonflower vines along their porches so that when they sat out at night they could enjoy the nocturnal bloom. ¶ On warm summer evenings the sweet fragrance of the 6-inch white flowers drifts through the still air, attracting singularly beautiful hawk moths, which hover around the blossoms like miniature hummingbirds. ¶ Aside from its romantic qualities, moonflower is a practical choice to provide shade or cover unsightly structures; the twining stems will climb at least 30 feet in a single season. ¶ **HOW TO DO IT** ¶ Sow your seeds indoors six to eight weeks before the last expected frost. Soak them overnight, then bury them 1 inch deep in potting mix (as described on p. 23). Seedlings emerge in seven to fifteen days. ¶ After the last chance of frost, you can safely plant the young vines outdoors. Transplant them when they are 4 to 6 inches tall. Make sure to harden them off for a week by leaving them outside in a protected area during the day and bringing them inside at night. Before planting, submerge the transplants in their containers in a sink or bucket of water until air bubbles cease to appear. ¶ In prepared garden soil that is thoroughly moist, dig a hole for each young plant that is at least twice as wide and twice as deep as the container. Space plants 6 inches apart. Gently remove a plant and its potting mix from the container, and set it in the hole so that the top of the root ball is just at soil level. Fill the holes with soil, packing it gently around the roots. Pat down the soil surface and water to fill in any air pockets. ¶ Guide the stems to the climbing structure with ties until they fasten on by themselves. Keep the soil moist but not soggy, and fertilize with a low-nitrogen liquid fertilizer every two weeks. Once the weather has warmed the ground, mulch each vine with 3 to 4 inches of organic compost in a circle 12 inches across.

Moonflower

Ipomoea alba

What You Need
Seeds
Containers to start seedlings
Potting mix
Up to 30 feet of wall, fence,
or other climbing structure
Plant ties
Low-nitrogen liquid fertilizer
Organic compost

Hardiness
Tender

Growing Conditions
1/2 day of direct sun

Climbing Method
Twining stems

When to Sow
Indoors 6 to 8 weeks before last frost

When to Prune
As necessary to control growth

When Blooms Appear
Summer

Seed and plant sources

This is a small sampling of reliable sources for vines. Some companies charge for their catalogue. Call first to check prices and availability.

J. L. Hudson, Seedsman
PO Box 1058
Redwood City, CA 94064
Loofah seeds. You must write for a catalogue.

Jackson and Perkins Roses
PO Box 1028
Medford, OR 97501
800 292-4769
Rugosa roses. They also carry some kits for climbing structures.

Ornamental Edibles
3622 Weedin Court
San Jose, CA 95132
408 946-SEED
Scarlet Runner beans and nasturtium seeds.

Petaluma Rose Company
581 Gossage Ave.
PO Box 750953
Petaluma, CA 94975
707 769-8862
Climbing 'Iceberg' roses.

Redwood City Seed Company
PO Box 361
Redwood City, CA 94064
415 325-7333
Scarlet runner beans, morning glories, and loofahs.

Seeds of Change
PO Box 15700
Santa Fe, NM 87506-5700
505 438-8080
Fax 505 438-7052
Scarlet runner beans and nasturtium.

Shepherd's Garden Seeds
6116 Highway 9
Felton, CA 95018
408 335-5216
Fax 408 335-2080
Seeds for scarlet runner beans, white pumpkin, nasturtium, and morning glories.

Sky Hoyt Specialty Grower
2650 Waldo Lane
Lakeport, CA 95453
707 279-0859
Twenty-four varieties of rare figs.

Thompson & Morgan
PO Box 1308
Jackson, NJ 08527
908 363-2225
Fax 908 363-9356
Seeds for moonflower and loofahs.

Materials Sources

Dalton Gazebos
20 Commerce Drive
Telford, PA 18969
215 721-1492
Prefabricated western red cedar gazebos, arbors, pergolas, and other garden structures.

Gardeners Eden
PO Box 7307
San Francisco, CA 94120-7307
800 822-9600
Metal and wood support structures for vines. Interesting metal trellises for containers.

Gazebo Woodcrafters
205 Virginia Street
Bellingham, WA 98225
206 734-0463
Gazebo kits for a weekend project.

Moultrie Manufacturing Co.
PO Drawer 1179
Moultrie, GA 31776-1179
800 841-8674
Kits for a variety of garden structures.

Smith and Hawken
25 Corte Madera
Mill Valley, CA 94941
415 383-4415
Wood and metal supports for climbing plants as well as some whimsical rustic structures.

BIBLIOGRAPHY

Bailey, L. H.
The Garden of Gourds.
New York: Macmillan, 1937.

Cox, Jeff.
Plant Marriages.
New York: HarperCollins, 1993.

Creasy, Rosalind.
Cooking from the Garden.
San Francisco: Sierra Club Books, 1988.

Hobhouse, Penelope.
Gardening Through the Ages.
New York: Simon & Schuster, 1992.

Hortus Third Dictionary.
New York: Macmillan, 1976.

Hottes, Alfred Carl.
Climbers and Groundcovers.
New York: de la Mare, 1947.

Kourik, Robert.
Designing Your Edible Landscape Naturally.
Santa Rosa, California:
Metamorphic Press, 1986.

Lacy, Allen.
Gardening with Groundcovers and Vines.
New York: HarperCollins,1993.

Strong, Roy.
The Garden Trellis.
New York: Simon & Schuster, 1991.

Sunset Western Garden Book.
Menlo Park, California:
Lane Publishing Company, 1990.

Taylor, Jane.
Climbing Plants: Kew Gardening Guide.
Portland, Oregon: Timber Press, 1987.

Whiteside, Katherine.
Antique Flowers.
New York: Villard Books, 1990.

INDEX

ACKNOWLEDGMENTS

This book, like a vine, grew and bloomed with the uplifting help and tender underpinning of many fellow gardeners, editors, and book crafters. ¶ We thank Jill Appenzeller for her professional advice as well as assistance in finding the beautiful vines we photographed. Anne Webster, Walter Strauss, Allison Zeremba, Rosalind Creasy, Bobbie Kinkead, Betsy Yates, Camilla Turnbull, Carol Reed, and Strybing Arboretum lent us the beauty of their garden visions. ¶ Hazel White, our wise-in-the-way-of-gardens editor, pruned, trimmed, and clipped to make the manuscript balanced and trim, as well as accurate and mannerly. ¶ Like the propensity of vines, we have leaned on the support and talents of Bill LeBlond, Leslie Jonath, Jill Jacobson, and David Carriere of Chronicle Books to provide the framework for success. We are grateful to our agents Susan Lescher and Mickey Choate from Lescher & Lescher, who assist us in untangling our publishing details. Thanks as well to Bob Aufuldish and Kathy Warinner, whose book design truly lifts us to graceful heights. And lastly to Arann and Daniel Harris, Mimi's own vines, whose blooms give the rarest pleasure.